THE
UNITED STATES, CUBA,
AND THE COLD WAR

American Failure
or Communist Conspiracy?

PROBLEMS IN AMERICAN CIVILIZATION

THE
UNITED STATES, CUBA,
AND THE COLD WAR

*American Failure
or Communist Conspiracy?*

EDITED WITH AN INTRODUCTION BY
Lester D. Langley
CENTRAL WASHINGTON STATE COLLEGE

D. C. HEATH AND COMPANY
Lexington, Massachusetts

CONTENTS

INTRODUCTION

THE postwar world has witnessed numerous Cold War crises—Berlin, Suez, and Korea—but none has proved more dangerous than the Soviet-American confrontation over Cuba in October, 1962. In what was a climactic moment in the Cold War two superpowers prepared to wage nuclear war.

What had precipitated the "Missile Crisis"? Observers noted that the immediate roots of the conflict lay in the Cuban-American clash that began with Fidel Castro's government in January, 1959. Castro's government decrees calling for nationalization of foreign-owned property, the circuslike trials of former Batista henchmen, and, finally, the Cuban dictator's avowal of Marxism-Leninism in December, 1961, laid the foundations for a Soviet satellite in the Americas. Those more sympathetic to Castro, of course, placed much of the blame for his defection to the Soviet bloc squarely on the United States. The American people had waged war against Spanish colonialism in 1898, they argued, but post-1898 policies relegated Cuba to a subservient role politically and economically. Castro merely liberated Cuba from the American orbit.

Fidel Castro symbolizes much of the anti-Americanism that inevitably accompanied the twentieth-century American imprint on Cuba. In the four years following Spain's defeat, United States military authorities ruled the island by right of conquest. In 1902 Cuba named its first president, but self-government came only when the Cuban assembly reluctantly adopted the Platt Amendment, by which Cuba provided a naval base for the United States, promised to limit its foreign debt, and agreed to sign no treaties impairing American interests. At the same time, the United States extended a preferential tariff on sugar, but this inevitably proved a curse, for Cuba remained subservient to a sugar economy. The industrial wealth of the island passed into foreign, principally American, ownership. In 1895, U.S. private investments in Cuba were $50 million; in 1925 they were approximately $1.5 billion!

Cuban dependence on the American economy continued until the overthrow of Fulgencio Batista in 1959, and the Castro propaganda machine has successfully exploited the issue by pointing to years of Yankee political manipulation in Cuban life. In 1906, the Theodore Roosevelt administration intervened, albeit reluctantly, and for three years Cubans lived under another military government. In 1917 and 1921 President Woodrow Wilson interfered in Cuban politics when one political party refused to abide by electoral results which it claimed were fraudulent. From 1925 to 1933 the American government recognized the despotic regime of Gerardo Machado, who probably surpassed Batista in the savage bestiality of his rule. In 1933, after years of assassinations, terrorist bombings, and strikes, Machado lost American support, and the island plunged into a political and economic maelstrom. The Franklin Roosevelt administration almost intervened with troops but decided to wait for the emergence of a capable leader who could guarantee public safety. From September, 1933, until January, 1934, the American government refused to recognize the reformist administration of Ramón Grau San Martín, a National University physician, who was described by special U.S. emissary Sumner Welles as a naïve visionary. Already, as later scholarship has revealed, the United States suspected a Communist plot in Cuba. Early in 1934 Fulgencio Batista, who had risen from the lowly position of clerk-stenographer in the Cuban army to a role of commanding political importance, made his move to support one of Grau's competitors. The new government, controlled by Batista, was recognized within a week. Batista was satisfied to remain as president-maker until 1940; he assumed the executive position in that year, but stepped down when his candidate was defeated in 1944. From 1944 to 1952 two civilians ruled Cuba, but the political process was not improved, and both governments, once in power, became tainted with rumors of graft and corruption. In March, 1952, Batista launched a *coup d'état* that toppled the government. From this moment Fidel Castro dedicated himself to the overthrow of Batista and the restoration of constitutional rule.

Thus, the acrimonious debate over Cuba involves a number of issues. Is Castroism the inevitable product of more than a century of American meddling in Cuba? Is Castro a Cuban revolutionary trying to erect a society that is truly independent economically and politically? Was Castro always a Communist, or was he driven into the Soviet bloc by the adamant American opposition to his brand of revolution? Finally, what is the impact of Castroism on American-Russian rivalry in world politics?

In Part I the nature of Castro's revolution is explored in four controversial pieces by Castro; Batista; Earl E. T. Smith, former ambassador to Cuba; and the late C. Wright Mills, a sociologist. Fidel Castro Ruz first drew international attention with his famous "History Will Absolve Me" speech in 1953, uttered before a Batista court trying him for a raid against the Moncada barracks in Santiago. Castro was sentenced to prison, but this speech, which he later lengthened into a revolutionary tract, marked his appearance as the spokesman for Cuban revolution. Castro promised to renovate the island's structure with political and economic reform. Between 1953 and 1959, many Cubans, who would later repudiate Castro's Marxism-Leninism, joined with his struggle to restore democracy to Cuba.

As the excerpts illustrate, the assignment of responsibility for Castro's success is as debatable as his profession of Marxism. Batista and Smith adopt the view, which many Americans accept, that Castro was *always* a Marxist convert but won public support in the United States because a favorable press paraded him as the "bearded warrior of the Sierra Maestra." Smith elaborates on the conspiracy theory by centering responsibility in the Department of State, particularly the Fourth Floor, where, Smith argues, there labored liberal intellectuals who wanted Castro to assume power. Smith's work easily fits into the genre of Cold War literature that has a fixation on conspiracies at home. Mills is more sympathetic to the early difficulties of Castro's government, arguing that social-economic injustices in Latin America led to Castroite upheavals. Thus, in the eyes of Mills and other critics of American policy, Castro had no choice but to erect a totalitarian state in order to achieve the benefits of revolution.

Part II contains a series of documents that trace the Cuban-American confrontation from 1959 to 1962. When Castro entered triumphantly into Havana in January, 1959, he was hailed by many in the United States as a new hope for Cuban democracy. The Castroite revolution, however, soon proved unpalatable to the American government and public. Foreign-controlled businesses complained of harsh treatment at the hands of Castro's ministers, and many Americans were shocked by the vengeful revolutionary justice meted out to former Batista associates. The diplomatic rupture occurred during a controversy over the staff at the American embassy in Havana. Annoyed, the Dwight D. Eisenhower administration announced its decision to terminate diplomatic relations. Shortly after the Eisenhower statement, the Cuban representative to the United Nations made serious charges against the United States in a speech before the Security Council. The Cuban revolution was now an international *cause célèbre*.

The next selections present the attitudes and arguments of American, Cuban, and Soviet officials who challenged each other during 1960–1962. In the first three excerpts, the Eisenhower administration attempts to justify its rejection of Castro's government on the grounds that Castro failed to abide by the precepts of international law in nationalizing foreign-owned property in Cuba. At the time, the United States also vigorously denied that it was abetting the overthrow of Castro's government. In fact, while the Eisenhower team planned to terminate diplomatic relations, the plans for an invasion of the island by exile groups, financed with American money, were well underway.

In an emotional address at the United Nations in January, 1961, the Cuban Minister of Foreign Relations, Raúl Roa, warned the Security Council that the United States was plotting an invasion of Cuba. Already, the Castro government had developed an appealing defense: a powerful United States was trying to destroy a militarily impotent but determined anti-imperialistic government in the Western Hemisphere. During the same session the United States, represented by James Wadsworth, was expanding on its counterclaim: Castroism was incompatible with hemispheric political and economic principles and was striving to initiate guerrilla war throughout the Americas.

Both the Cuban and the American contentions contained elements of truth. An invasion *was* being planned; Castro *was* fomenting guerrilla activity throughout the Caribbean. The spirited debate of early January was followed by the inauguration of John Fitzgerald Kennedy and the Bay of Pigs debacle of April. Kennedy was naturally suspicious of the invasion plans but, informed that it was "now or never" and that the exiles were becoming restless in their Central American bases, eventually gave his approval. The humiliating military defeat of the invaders was surpassed only by the diplomatic defeat of the United States, universally scorned, its image marred throughout the Americas.

As the next readings show, the Soviet Union leaped at the opportunity to condemn "American aggression," and Kennedy felt impelled to defend his Cuban record. His April 20 speech to the American Society of Newspaper Editors, given shortly after the Bay of Pigs defeat, was a courageous admission of his own misjudgment and a warning to the Soviet Union that the U.S. would not tolerate Communist penetration of the hemisphere. Kennedy was already trying to identify the United States with Latin America's nonviolent progressive elements by his espousal of the Alliance for Progress. But, clearly, the Bay of Pigs was the blackest day for American policy in Latin America since Theodore Roosevelt "took" Panama in 1903.

Throughout the year Castro boasted of his triumph and added to the humiliation by his excessive demands for the repatriation of the Bay of Pigs prisoners. In December came his announcement of conversion to Marxism-Leninism. The initial bonds with the Soviet Union had appeared already in a variety of trade agreements. Unknown to the American government was the infamous "missile pact" signed by Castro and Nikita Khrushchev. Historians are unsure about the origins of this agreement: Castro may have demanded nuclear protection as insurance against another Bay of Pigs; or Khrushchev, severely criticized by the Chinese, may have been gambling that the U.S.S.R. could alter the nuclear balance of power. Cuban exiles and several congressmen gave repeated warnings of suspicious activity in the Cuban countryside in mid-1962, but it was not until October that Kennedy associates confirmed the presence of missile placements. For two grim weeks in October, the U.S. and the U.S.S.R. prepared for a nuclear showdown.

The following selections recount these tense days beginning with the President's memorable October 22 "quarantine" speech to the nation. In the next excerpt, the President's brother, Attorney General Robert Kennedy, relates

how the "quarantine" decision came
about and the agonizing hours that
were spent debating the military alternatives and political and moral considerations which the United States confronted in the crisis. This selection,
from Robert Kennedy's posthumously
published memoir, is valuable for an
understanding of the "inner working"
of the special task force that dealt
with the missile crisis.

In the United Nations, the representatives of the three antagonists—Adlai
Stevenson, Mario García-Incháustegui,
and Valerian Zorin—debated the Cold
War issue of Cuba. During the Bay of
Pigs crisis, Stevenson had dutifully de-
fended a weak American case; his
speech during the missile crisis was a
rhetorical tour de force. Part II con-
cludes with the Cuban and Soviet coun-
terarguments and some selections from
the Kennedy-Khrushchev correspondence
on the removal of the missiles.

Part III is concerned with the impact
of Castroism on the Cold War and the
reaction of the United States. Scholars
differ on the degree of American responsibility for the Cuban debacle and
the nature of Castro's threat to the underdeveloped world, especially Latin
America. Did the U.S. forget its revolutionary past by condemning Castro,
thus driving him into the Soviet camp?
In the first selection, William A. Williams, a diplomatic historian often associated with "new left" political attitudes, sees Castro's defection to the
Soviet bloc not as the working of a
Communist conspiracy but as the
inevitable culmination of American harassment and refusal to adjust to revolutionary dynamism. Williams, a per-
ceptive analyst of American foreign
policy, has written at length on the
failure of the United States to recognize
its hypocrisy in dealing with twentieth-
century upheaval. American leaders and
policymakers, he contends, are blind to
the nationalistic and xenophobic character of modern revolution.

Williams' analysis of the Cuban question is paired with a selection from
Arthur   Schlesinger's   prize-winning
memoir of the Kennedy years, A Thousand Days. Like Williams, Schlesinger
is a historian, but his previous works
have focused on American politics,
particularly the New Deal. During the
Kennedy Presidency, he was heavily involved in the Latin American theater.
At that time the issue of Cuba posed
something of an intellectual quandary:
the Kennedy program was anti-Castro,
but it was also supposed to be aligned
with the Latin American nonviolent
left. The Bay of Pigs fiasco brought
angry charges from liberals that the
New Frontier intellectuals preached reform in Latin America but practiced
power   politics.   In   this   selection,
Schlesinger deftly argues that although
Kennedy made mistakes, his overall
policy in Latin America, as expressed in
the Alliance for Progress, was a progressive, rational plea for social change and
a viable alternative to the violence
preached by Castro.

The case of Cuba is an excellent il-
lustration of the Cold War dilemmas
facing the United States in the Third
World. Our recent experience with Castro and Castro's revolution embodies
muddled diplomacy, confused thinking,
lost hopes, and conspiratorial night-
mares. Castro's threat is more than
military, for in rejecting Castroism in
Latin America, the United States often
finds itself uncomfortably at the side of
the old order. Yet the dissipation of the
earlier atmosphere of crisis suggests
that all three nations—Cuba, the United
States, and the Soviet Union—have
learned some lessons that may serve to
reduce other points of tension in world
politics.

CONFLICT OF OPINION

Cuba should be the bulwark of liberty and not a shameful link in the chain of despotism.

—FIDEL CASTRO

There is a limit to what the United States in self-respect can endure. That limit has now been reached. Our friendship for the Cuban people is not affected. It is my hope and my conviction that in the not too distant future it will be possible for the historic friendship between us once again to find its reflection in normal relations of every sort. Meanwhile, our sympathy goes out to the people of Cuba now suffering under the yoke of a dictator.

—PRESIDENT DWIGHT D. EISENHOWER

The blindest and most powerful enemy of the Cuban revolution has been and is the imperialist Government and reactionary group headed by President Eisenhower.

—RAÚL ROA

The Soviet Government reserves the right, if armed intervention in the affairs of the Cuban people is not stopped, to take all measures with other countries to render the necessary assistance to the Republic of Cuba.

—SOVIET RESPONSE TO THE BAY OF PIGS

. . . The Castro propaganda mill cleverly imputed its own crimes to its victims. The forces of law and order became the murderers and sadists. These big lies were shrewdly disseminated by a minority of U.S. publicists who, wittingly or unwittingly, served the Communist cause with unswerving consistency and consummate guile.

—FULGENCIO BATISTA

The day-by-day actions of those on the Fourth Floor of the State Department shaped United States–Latin American foreign policy as far as Cuba was concerned.

—EARL E. T. SMITH

The United States quickly interpreted Castro's actions of late 1959, and his trade deal with the Soviet Union early in 1960, as meaning that Cuba had become a totalitarian Communist satellite. Most commentators have followed that official government line. Neither claim is factually correct.

—WILLIAM A. WILLIAMS

With some trepidation, I argued that, whatever validity the military and political arguments were for an attack in preference to a blockade, America's traditions and history would not permit such a course of action. . . . Our struggle against Communism throughout the world was far more than physical survival—it had as its essence our heritage and our ideals, and these we must not destroy.

—ROBERT F. KENNEDY

I. CASTRO'S REVOLUTION

Fidel Castro

HISTORY WILL ABSOLVE ME

On July 26, 1953, Castro and a handful of guerrillas attacked the Moncada barracks in Santiago de Cuba. The survivors were captured, and Castro was tried before an emergency tribunal on October 16. Convicted in a Batista-controlled court, Castro was sentenced to prison on the Isle of Pines and released in an amnesty two years later. After training in Mexico, he led another band into the Sierra Maestra of Cuba in 1956. From his mountain stronghold, Castro directed a guerrilla war against the Batista dictatorship until January 1, 1959, when Batista fled Cuba and Castro became leader. *History Will Absolve Me*, a revision of Castro's original defense plea in 1953, soon was lauded as a basic document in the Castroite revolutionary program.

As soon as Santiago de Cuba was in our hands, we would immediately have readied the people for war. Bayamo was attacked precisely to situate our advance forces along the Cauto River. Never forget that this province which has a million and a half inhabitants today, provides without a doubt the best resistance and the most patriotic men of Cuba. It was this province that continued the fight for independence for thirty years and paid the highest tribute in blood, sacrifice and heroism. In Oriente, you can still breathe the air of that glorious epoch. At dawn, when the cocks crow as if they were bugles calling soldiers to reveille, and when the sun rises, radiant, over the rugged mountains, it seems that once again we will hear the cry of Yara or Baire.[1]

I stated that the second consideration on which we based our chances for success was one of social order because we were assured of the people's support. When we speak of the people we do not mean the comfortable ones, the conservative elements of the nation, who welcome any regime of oppression, any dictatorship, any despotism, prostrating themselves before the master of the moment until they grind their foreheads into the ground. When we speak of struggle, the *people* means the vast unredeemed masses, to whom all make promises and whom all deceive; we mean the people who yearn for a better, more dignified and more just nation; who are moved by ancestral aspirations of justice, for they have suffered injustice and mockery, generation after generation; who long for great and wise changes in all aspects of their life; people, who, to attain these changes, are ready to give even the very last breath of their lives— when they believe in something or in someone, especially when they believe in themselves. In stating a purpose, the first condition of sincerity and good faith, is to do precisely what nobody else ever does, that is, to speak with absolute clarity, without fear. The demagogues and professional politicians who manage to perform the miracle of being right in everything and in pleasing everyone, are, of necessity, deceiving ev-

[1] *Yara and Baire.* "Yara" on October 10, 1868, was the first battle cry for independence. The cry of "Baire" on February 24, 1895, announced the final drive to liberate Cuba from Spanish rule.

From Fidel Castro, *History Will Absolve Me* (Havana: Cooperativa Obrera de Publicidad, 1960), pp. 33–40, 78–79.

eryone about everything. The revolutionaries must proclaim their ideas courageously, define their principles and express their intentions so that no one is deceived, neither friend nor foe.

The people we counted on in our struggle were these:

Seven hundred thousand Cubans without work, who desire to earn their daily bread honestly without having to emigrate in search of livelihood.

Five hundred thousand farm laborers inhabiting miserable shacks, who work four months of the year and starve for the rest of the year, sharing their misery with their children, who have not an inch of land to cultivate, and whose existence inspires compassion in any heart not made of stone.

Four hundred thousand industrial laborers and stevedores whose retirement funds have been embezzled, whose benefits are being taken away, whose homes are wretched quarters, whose salaries pass from the hands of the boss to those of the usurer, whose future is a pay reduction and dismissal, whose life is eternal work and whose only rest is in the tomb.

One hundred thousand small farmers who live and die working on land that is not theirs, looking at it with sadness as Moses did the promised land, to die without possessing it; who, like feudal serfs, have to pay for the use of their parcel of land by giving up a portion of their products; who cannot love it, improve it, beautify it or plant a lemon or an orange tree on it, because they never know when a sheriff will come with the rural guard to evict them from it.

Thirty thousand teachers and professors who are so devoted, dedicated and necessary to the better destiny of future generations and who are so badly treated and paid.

Twenty thousand small businessmen weighted down by debts, ruined by the crisis and harangued by a plague of filibusters and venal officials.

Ten thousand young professionals: doctors, engineers, lawyers, veterinarians, school teachers, dentists, pharmacists, newspapermen, painters, sculptors, etc., who come forth from school with their degrees, anxious to work and full of hope, only to find themselves at a dead end with all doors closed, and where no ear hears their clamor or supplication.

These are the people, the ones who know misfortune and, therefore, are capable of fighting with limitless courage!

To the people whose desperate roads through life have been paved with the brick of betrayals and false promises, we were not going to say: "we will eventually give you what you need, but rather —Here you have it, fight for it with all your might so that liberty and happiness may be yours!"

In the brief of this cause there must be recorded the five revolutionary laws that would have been proclaimed immediately after the capture of the Moncada barracks and would have been broadcast to the nation by radio. It is possible that Colonel Chaviano may deliberately have destroyed these documents, but even if he has done so, I conserve them in my memory.

The First Revolutionary Law would have returned power to the people and proclaimed the Constitution of 1940 the supreme Law of the land, until such time as the people should decide to modify or change it. And, in order to effect its implementation and punish those who had violated it—there being no organization for holding elections to accomplish this—the revolutionary movement, as the momentous incarnation of this sovereignty, the only source of legitimate power, would have assumed all the faculties inherent to it, except that of modifying the Constitution itself: in other words it would have assumed the legislative, executive and judicial powers.

This approach could not be more crystal clear nor more free of vacillation and sterile charlatanry. A government acclaimed by the mass of rebel people would be vested with every power, everything necessary in order to proceed with the effective implementation of the popular will and true justice. From that moment, the Judicial Power, which since March 10th has placed itself *against* the Constitution and *outside* the Constitution, would cease to exist and we would proceed to its immediate and total reform before it would again assume the power granted to it by the Supreme Law of the Republic. Without our first taking those previous measures, a return to legality by putting the custody of the courts back into the hands that have crippled the system so dishonorably would constitute a fraud, a deceit, and one more betrayal.

The Second Revolutionary Law would have granted property, not mortgageable and not transferable, to all planters, sub-planters, lessees, partners and squatters who hold parcels of five or less "caballerias"[2] of land, and the state would indemnify the former owners on the basis of the rental which they would have received for these parcels over a period of ten years.

The Third Revolutionary Law would have granted workers and employees the right to share 30% of the profits of all the large industrial, mercantile and mining enterprises, including the sugar mills. The strictly agricultural enterprises would be exempt in consideration of other agrarian laws which would have been implemented.

The Fourth Revolutionary Law would have granted all planters the right to share 55% of the sugar production and a minimum quota of forty thousand "arrobas"[3] for all small planters who have been established for three or more years.

The Fifth Revolutionary Law would have ordered the confiscation of all holdings and ill-gotten gains of those who had committed frauds during previous regimes, as well as the holdings and ill-gotten gains of all their legatees and heirs. To implement this, special courts with full powers would gain access to all records of all corporations registered or operating in this country [in order] to investigate concealed funds of illegal origin, and to request that foreign governments extradite persons and attach holdings [rightfully belonging to the Cuban people]. Half of the property recovered would be used to subsidize retirement

funds for workers and the other half would be used for hospitals, asylums and charitable organizations.

Furthermore, it was to be declared that the Cuban policy in the Americas would be one of close solidarity with the democratic people of this continent, and that those politically persecuted by bloody tyrants oppressing our sister nations would find generous asylum, brotherhood, and bread in the land of Martí. Not the persecution, hunger and treason that they find today. Cuba should be the bulwark of liberty and not a shameful link in the chain of despotism.

These laws would have been proclaimed immediately, as soon as the upheaval was ended and prior to a detailed and far-reaching study, they would have been followed by another series of laws and fundamental measures, such as, the Agrarian Reform, Integral Reform of Education, nationalization of the Utilities Trust and the Telephone Trust, refund to the people of the illegal excessive rates this company has charged, and payment to the Treasury of all taxes brazenly evaded in the past.

All these laws and others would be inspired in the exact fulfillment of two essential articles of our Constitution. One of these orders the outlawing of feudal estates by indicating the maximum area of land any person or entity can possess for each type of agricultural enterprise, by adopting measures which would tend to revert the land to the Cubans. The other categorically orders the State to use all means at its disposal to provide employment to all those who lack it and to insure a decent livelihood to each manual laborer or intellectual.

None of these articles may be called unconstitutional. The first popularly elected government would have to respect these laws, not only because of moral obligation to the nation, but because when people achieve something they have yearned for throughout generations, no force in the world is capable of taking it away again.

The problems concerning land, the problem of industrialization, the problem of housing, the problem of unem-

---

[2] *Caballeria.* tract of land, about 33 1/3 acres.
[3] *Arroba.* 25 pounds.

ployment, the problem of education and the problem of the health of the people; these are the six problems we would take immediate steps to resolve, along with the restoration of public liberties and political democracy.

Perhaps this exposition appears cold and theoretical if one does not know the shocking and tragic conditions of the country with regard to these six problems, to say nothing of the most humiliating political oppression.

85% of the small farmers in Cuba pay rent and live under the constant threat of being dispossessed from the land that they cultivate. More than half the best cultivated land belongs to foreigners. In *Oriente*, the largest province, the lands of the United Fruit Company and West Indian Company join the north coast to the southern one. There are two hundred thousand peasant families who do not have a single acre of land to cultivate to provide food for their starving children. On the other hand, nearly three hundred thousand "caballerias" of productive land owned by powerful interests remains uncultivated.

Cuba is above all an agricultural state. Its population is largely rural. The city depends on these rural areas. The rural people won the Independence. The greatness and prosperity of our country depends on a healthy and vigorous rural population that loves the land and knows how to cultivate it, within the framework of a state that protects and guides them. Considering all this, how can the present state of affairs be tolerated any longer?

With the exception of a few food, lumber and textile industries, Cuba continues to be a producer of raw materials. We export sugar to import candy, we export hides to import shoes, we export iron to import plows. Everybody agrees that the need to industrialize the country is urgent, that we need steel industries, paper and chemical industries; that we must improve cattle and grain products, the technique and the processing in our food industry, in order to balance the ruinous competition of the Europeans in cheese products, condensed milk, liquors and oil, and that of the

Americans in canned goods; that we need merchant ships; that tourism should be an enormous source of revenue. But the capitalists insist that the workers remain under a Claudian[4] yoke; the State folds its arms and industrialization can wait for the Greek calends.

Just as serious or even worse is the housing problem. There are two hundred thousand huts and hovels in Cuba; four hundred thousand families in the country and in the cities live cramped into barracks and tenements without even the minimum sanitary requirements; two million two hundred thousand of our urban population pay rents which absorb between one fifth and one third of their income; and two million eight hundred thousand of our rural and suburban population lack electricity. If the State proposes lowering rents, landlords threaten to freeze all construction; if the State does not interfere, construction goes on so long as the landlords get high rents, otherwise, they would not lay a single brick even though the rest of the population should have to live exposed to the elements. The utilities monopoly is no better: they extend lines as far as it is profitable and beyond that point, they don't care if the people have to live in darkness for the rest of their lives. The State folds its arms and the people have neither homes nor electricity.

Our educational system is perfectly compatible with the rest of our national situation. Where the *guajiro*[5] is not the owner of his land, what need is there for agricultural schools? Where there are no industries what need is there for technical or industrial schools? Everything falls within the same absurd logic: there is neither one thing nor the other. In any small European country there are more than 200 technical and industrial arts schools; in Cuba, there are only six such schools, and the boys graduate without having anywhere to use their skills. The little rural schools are attended by only half the school-age chil-

[4] *Claudius Caecus.* refers to Roman Emperor who so oppressed the plebeians that they left Rome.
[5] *Guajiro.* term usually refers to modest and underprivileged farmers in *Oriente* province.

dren—barefoot, half-naked and under-nourished—and frequently the teacher must buy necessary materials from his own salary. Is this the way to make a nation great?

Only death can liberate one from so much misery. In this, however,—early death—the state is most helpful. 90% of rural children are consumed by parasites which filter through their bare feet from the earth. Society is moved to compassion upon hearing of the kidnapping or murder of one child, but they are criminally indifferent to the mass murder of so many thousands of children who die every year from lack of facilities, agonizing with pain. Their innocent eyes—death already shining in them—seem to look into infinity as if entreating forgiveness for human selfishness, as if asking God to stay his wrath. When the head of a family works only four months a year, with what can he purchase clothing and medicine for his children? They will grow up with rickets, with not a single good tooth in their mouths by the time they reach thirty; they will have heard ten million speeches and will finally die of misery and deception. Public hospitals, which are always full, accept only patients recommended by some powerful politician who, in turn, demands the electoral votes of the unfortunate one and his family so that Cuba may continue forever the same or worse.

With this background, is it not understandable that from May to December over a million persons lost their jobs, and that Cuba, with a population of five and a half million, has a greater percentage of unemployed than France or Italy with a population of forty million each?

When you judge a defendant for robbery, Your Honors, do you ask him how long he has been unemployed? Do you ask him how many children he has, which days of the week he ate and which he didn't, do you concern yourselves with his environment at all? You send him to jail without further thought. But those who burn warehouses and stores to collect insurance do not go to jail, even though a few human beings should have happened to [be cremated with the property insured]. The insured have

money to hire lawyers and bribe judges. You jail the poor wretch who steals because he is hungry; but none of the hundreds who steal from the Government has ever spent a night in jail; you dine with them at the end of the year in some elegant place and they enjoy your respect.

In Cuba when a bureaucrat becomes a millionaire overnight and enters the fraternity of the rich, he could very well be greeted with the words of that opulent Balzac character, Taillefer, who, in his toast to the young heir to an enormous fortune, said: "Gentlemen, let us drink to the power of gold! Mr. Valentine, a millionaire six times over has just ascended the throne. He is king, can do everything, is above everything—like all the rich. Henceforward, equality before the law, before the Constitution, will be a myth for him; for he will not be subject to laws, the laws will be subject to him. There are no courts or sentences for millionaires."

The future of the country and the solution of its problems cannot continue to depend on the selfish interests of a dozen financiers, nor on the cold calculations of profits that ten or twelve magnates draw up in their air-conditioned offices. The country cannot continue begging on its knees for miracles from a few golden calves, similar to the Biblical one destroyed by the fury of a prophet. Golden calves cannot perform miracles of any kind. The problems of the Republic can be solved only if we dedicate ourselves to fight for that Republic with the same energy, honesty and patriotism our liberators had when they created it.

I come to the close of my defense plea but I will not end it as lawyers usually do —asking that the accused be freed. I cannot ask freedom for myself while my comrades are suffering in the ignominious prison of *Isla de Pinos*. Send me there to join them and to share their fate. It is understandable that honest men should be dead or in prison in [this] Republic where the president is a criminal and a thief.

To the Honorable Magistrates, my sincere gratitude for having allowed me to express myself freely without petty interruptions, I hold no bitterness toward you. I recognize that in certain aspects you have been humane and I know that the Presiding Officer of this court, a man of unimpeachable private life, cannot disguise his repugnance at the current state of affairs that oblige him to dictate unjust decisions.

Still, there remains for this hearing a more serious problem, the issues arising from the murder of seventy men—that is to say, the greatest massacre we have ever known. The guilty continue at liberty with a weapon in hand—a weapon which continually threatens the citizens. If all the weight of the law does not fall upon [the guilty] because of cowardice, or because of domination of the courts —and if then, all the magistrates and judges do not resign, I pity you. And I regret the unprecedented shame that will fall over the judicial system.

I know that imprisonment will be as hard for me as it has ever been for anyone—filled with cowardly threats and wicked torture. But I do not fear prison, just as I do not fear the fury of the miserable tyrant who snuffed life out of 70 brothers of mine.

Sentence me. I don't mind. *History will absolve me.*

Fulgencio Batista

THE RISE OF CASTRO

Batista ruled Cuba as President and President-maker from 1934 until 1944. In March, 1952, he engineered a *coup d'état* that ousted the government of Carlos Prío Socarrás. In this selection, written while in exile in Portugal, Batista justifies the coup as an attempt to prevent the erection of a Cuban Communist state.

AFTER March 10, 1952, I felt it was necessary to limit the time and scope of the emergency powers that flowed from the bloodless revolution. From the outset, I explained that I had no desire to perpetuate myself in office. We prepared the means for a smooth transition from the extraordinary regime to a normal democratic one. Article 254 of the Constitutional Law enacted on April 4th provided for general elections and required the Cabinet to specify within 60 days the offices to be filled and their length of tenure.

The Electoral College was assigned the task of proposing revisions in the Electoral Code and of promulgating regulations based upon the Code. The impartiality of that 1943 Code could scarcely be challenged by my opponents since it had governed the 1944 elections in which my political group was defeated by the Auténticos under [Ramón] Grau San Martín.

To give greater scope to political activity and to ensure that the vote of the people would determine the Government, a Constitutional Reform was drafted. This was to be submitted to referendum at the time of the election with the understanding that, if it should be defeated, the 1940 Constitution would automatically be reinstated upon the inauguration of the next President.

These procedures were closely parallel to those we had resorted to during the

From Fulgencio Batista, *The Growth and the Decline of the Cuban Republic*, trans. Blas M. Rocafort (New York, 1964), pp. 38–49. Copyright © 1964 by the Devin-Adair Company. Reprinted by permission of the publisher. Documenting footnotes in this and subsequent selections have been omitted.

transition from the revolutionary regimes arising out of the overthrow of the [Gerardo] Machado Government [in 1933] to the Administrations elected under the 1940 Constitution. During that interim period, four electoral codes had been enacted and three Censuses carried out so that we would have a complete and accurate roster of eligible voters. Our Revolution summoned the people three times to vote for a President, Governors, Mayors, Senators and Aldermen, five times for Congressmen and once for delegates to a Constitutional Convention.

Within the time set by law, the Government specified the elective offices to be filled. Law #105 of June 2, 1952 defined the procedures for the election of a President, a Vice President, a Senate of 54 members, at least a third of whom must represent minority parties, a House of Representatives with one member for every 45,000 inhabitants and also Governors, Mayors and Aldermen.

The Electoral College submitted a proposed Electoral Code to the Cabinet on schedule. The draft law strengthened our democratic institutions and, by making split-ticket voting impossible in many instances, tended to make parties and programs more important than the personalities of the individual candidates.

The realization of this transition was blocked by the intolerance of the opposition political organizations, which preferred to abstain from the elections to admitting the existence of the revolutionary government. Because of this intransigent attitude, we were obliged to move the date of the proposed election forward to 1954. While the motivation for abstention was the well-justified fear by the opposition that it would be defeated at the polls, my associates and I were determined to do everything possible to have an electoral contest in which the voters would be free to vote for the opposition parties as well as for our own.

THE MONCADA ASSAULT

The country was at peace; order reigned; the people enjoyed complete liberty; there seemed to be general support of the Government. At this time, in midsummer of 1953, the people of Santiago de Cuba were enjoying the carnival and had little thought of politics. In this atmosphere of peace, a sudden, unprovoked surprise attack on the soldiers of the Moncada Barracks in the city took place. The assault began in the early hours of July 26, 1953, a Sunday when the troops were either enjoying the carnival in the city or sleeping off their revelries.

The attack was led by Fidel and Raúl Castro and other Communists. It began with the assassination of sick men in their beds in the hospital clinic adjoining the camp. Sentinels and soldiers sleeping in their beds were also murdered. The troops fought back, killed a number of their assailants and easily restored complete control over the barracks.

Fidel Castro, the organizer of the attack, did not appear at the scene of the fighting. Both during, and for several days after, the murders, which he and his Communist superiors had planned, he remained hidden in town. When it was safe to do so, he emerged under the protection of Monsignor Enrique Pérez Serantes, Archbishop of Santiago de Cuba.

Orders were given to respect Castro's life. In accordance with the democratic principles of my Administration, he was tried in an ordinary civilian court before independent judges, at least one of whom was hostile to the regime.

At the time Castro arrived in Santiago to help plan the operation, eight of the top ranking leaders of Cuban communism, among them Lázaro Peña and Joaquín Ordoqui, slipped into Santiago. Later, at the trial, they alleged that they had come to the city to celebrate the birthday of their leader, Blas Roca, the General Secretary of the Party. This was a transparent falsification, both because Blas Roca lived in Havana and because Communist functionaries are not sentimental enough to take a round trip of over a thousand miles because of a birthday party. Moreover, the Party had been outlawed and its leaders had either fled abroad or were in hiding. Under these circumstances, they would only have travelled to Santiago de Cuba for a most important reason. That reason was to plan the attack on the Moncada Barracks.

Castro was sentenced to 15 years in prison. He began to serve his term on the Isle of Pines which, under his dictatorship, has become the worst hell hole in the Western Hemisphere. Under my Administration, however, Fidel Castro, as a political prisoner, was given a pavilion to live in, the use of a jeep with chauffeur, full access to whatever books he chose to read and complete freedom to write whatever he wanted to.

In prison, Castro continued with his monstrous deception. Writing to Dr. Luis Conte Agüero on December 12, 1953 from prison, he observed: "Our triumph would have meant the immediate rise of the Orthodox Party to power. . . . Speak to Dr. Agramonte, show him this letter, express to him our loyal sentiments. . . ." To his Communist associates, Castro sang another tune. On April 17, 1954, he wrote Melba Hernández, one of those who had used cold steel in the Moncada attack:

"Use guile and smiles with everyone. Follow the same tactics we followed at the trial: defend our point of view without irritating anyone. There will be more than enough time later to trample all of the cockroaches together. Accept any help offered, but remember to trust no one. . . ."

RETURN TO THE BALLOT BOXES

The cowardly attack on the Moncada Barracks forced the Government to take exceptional measures and to suspend certain guarantees as provided for in the Cuban Constitution. The elections had to be postponed, but the political parties could carry on their activities at will.

To ensure complete fairness, we invited all the political parties and factions to discuss the new Electoral Code which would govern the forthcoming Presidential elections of November 1, 1954.

A few hours before the polls were opened and at a time when all the election boards had been named, Dr. Grau San Martín, the candidate of the Cuban Revolutionary Party, requested a postponement of the balloting. The matter was debated on television and radio. The Electoral College decided that Dr. Grau's complaints were without foundation and it was generally realized that he was concerned with obstructing the democratic process for the simple reason that he had no chance of winning.

Grau withdrew and ordered the candidates of his party to do likewise. Nevertheless, the people went to the polls in droves. I was elected President of Cuba for the second time and, despite their leader's directive, several Cuban Revolutionary Party (PRC) candidates were elected to Congress.

My inauguration in February 1954 as Constitutional President of Cuba was attended by special envoys from 51 countries. The growth of Cuba's international prestige was clearly evident. For our part, we maintained cordial relations with all the nations of the world with the exception of the Communist countries.

At the end of eight years of persecution, four of which were spent in exile, our second constitutional government began in an aura of peace and work. The fundamental objective was to carry out a great program for economic and social development, one which was already under way. I hoped that Cuba would continue to set an example in advanced social legislation for the Americas.

The opposition was divided into two groups: those who favored attaining power through peaceful and constitutional means and those who refused all compromise, abstained from the polls and were prepared to use conspiracy, assassination, sabotage and terror to win supreme power for themselves.

AMNESTY

The times were not propitious for an amnesty of all political prisoners, but my supporters in Congress and I hoped that an act of great clemency and generosity which opened the prison doors to the terrorists might convince some of them to become normal human beings, to do something useful for society and to confine their political opposition to the channels prescribed by law.

The general amnesty was issued and the Castro brothers, among others, were freed under it. After loudly announcing his intention to repeat his treasonable attack on the State, Fidel Castro proceeded openly to Mexico to prepare there to carry out his purpose.

CONSULTATIVE COUNCIL

Although my Government had been invested with extraordinary powers by the fact of revolution, I did not want to exercise the legislative power without first hearing public opinion. Therefore, as soon as the Revolution had consolidated its power, I created a new organism, consisting of outstanding men and women who represented the manifold activities of the nation. It was called the Consultative Council and was composed of 80 members and 15 alternates.

Among other powers, it had the right to propose laws, to be heard on basic matters of government and to intervene in fiscal matters and international relations through its commissions and its plenary sessions. All of its proposals, once they had been discussed and approved, were submitted to the Council of Ministers for final action. The members of the Council had the untrammeled right to express their opinions and vote as their consciences dictated. They enjoyed a protection tantamount to parliamentary immunity.

The most important organizations of the nation were represented on the Council by their most prominent members. This included, for example, the Presidents of the Associations of Sugar Mill Owners and of Sugar Planters, the Secretary General of the Cuban Confederation of Labor (CTC) and of the National Federation of Sugar Workers (FNTA), the leaders of other federations and labor unions, agrarian leaders, veterans of the War of Independence, farmers, economists, landowners, industrialists, former Ministers, legislators and mayors. No other deliberative body ever represented the nation as well.

The Consultative Council was called into session on 168 occasions and there were only ten times when it was unable to meet because of lack of a quorum. It met weekly in plenary session, dedicating the rest of its time to the study by its many commissions of the various projects placed before it. The constitutional principle of not passing on any legislation without at least one report from one of its commissions was strictly observed. Before acting on its recommendations, the proposed legislation was discussed in hearings at which interested groups were heard. This system, which was rigorously adhered to, assured that all interested groups would be able to state their case and, on occasion, secure modifications before laws were enacted.

The Council had four Presidents: Drs. Carlos Saladrigas Zayas, Gastón Godoy Loret de Mola, Justo García Rayneri and General of the Armies of Liberation Generoso Campos Marquetti. Each of these men left the Council in order to form part of the Cabinet.

THE CIVIC DIALOGUES

In the beginning of 1956, efforts were made to bring about an agreement or *modus vivendi* between the opposition and the Government. Meetings were organized by the Society of Friends of the Republic, composed of semi-neutrals and opponents of the Administration: the Orthodox Party to which Castro belonged, the Prío faction of the Auténticos, which favored conspiracy and violence, and the Auténticos of Grau who favored a solution at the polls.

These conferences were called Civic Dialogues. They were presided over by the eighty-year-old patrician, Cosme de la Torriente, a Colonel of the War of Independence. No agreement could be reached because the radicals insisted, as their first condition, that the Government resign. We did not reject this demand out of hand, but proposed instead that a Constituent Assembly with unlimited power be called to give the people the opportunity to decide whether the Government should resign or serve out its legal term until February 24, 1959. This counterproposal was rejected by the extremists, possibly because they were intimidated by Castro terrorists, and the discussions came to an end.

It is of some interest that, while Prío was negotiating at these Civic Dialogues and simulating a desire for peace, his henchmen made an attack on the Goicuria military camp in the city of Matanzas.

Despite the failure of the Civic Dialogues, we did everything in our power to help the opposition use legal and democratic channels. For example, the National Revolutionary Movement under Pardo Llada did not have enough registrations to qualify as a legal party. To encourage lawful opposition, Law #1307 of February 26, 1954 was passed so that it could qualify. However, when Pardo Llada saw he would not have enough support to win even a single seat for himself or his followers in the House of Representatives, he left for Spain on funds belonging to his party and then announced that he would return via the United States and enter the election campaign. Actually, he proceeded from New York to Venezuela, then appeared suddenly in the Sierra Maestra and served as Fidel Castro's privileged radio propagandist until 1961. In the latter year, on arriving in Mexico on a mission for his Government, he "deserted." The Mexican press was unanimously hostile and labelled him "the Minister of Hate."

ELECTIONS OF NOVEMBER 1958

The elections of November 1958 were held under horribly unfavorable conditions. With the consistent support of the United States Government and a dominant sector of the American press, the Castro movement was gaining strength by leaps and bounds. The American arms embargo on my Government was generally interpreted as a decision by Washington to support Castro's drive for power. Under these conditions, the morally weak, the venal and the opportunistic supported the bearded outlaw. When the State Department allowed Castro's Communist bands to kidnap American citizens without making any effective protest, a further demoralization of those forces in Cuba which believed in democracy and decency inevitably occurred.

A campaign of deceit and lies was unleashed by the men of the Sierra Maestra. Since they were determined to seize power for themselves with no competitors, it was necessary to their purpose that the scheduled elections should either not take place or else be discredited. Law #2 of the Sierra Maestra imposed the death penalty on all urban candidates in the election who refused to withdraw their candidacy. This death sentence could be imposed by members of the Rebel Army or by the so-called Castro militia. It applied to opposition candidates (including the candidates of what had supposedly been Castro's own political group, the Orthodox Party) as well as to my supporters. This law was nothing less than a general license to murder any Cuban who believed in democracy and good government enough to run for public office.

Terrorists' attacks increased. Coercion rose toward a zenith. Communications, schools, courthouses and trade union centers were demolished. Candidates, political leaders, party workers and others were murdered in their homes or on their way to work. To give a few examples from hundreds of cases: Nicolás Rivero Agüero, brother of the Presidential candidate of the pro-government forces, and also brother of Rebel leader Luis Conte Agüero, was assassinated; Felipe Navea, Vice President of the National Maritime Union, was killed in the presence of his wife; the teacher-candidate for Congress, Aníbal Vega Vega, was killed on his doorstep; and cattleman Rosendo Collazo was murdered at his ranch in the presence of his wife by a group of outlaws wearing 26th of July armbands and led by his former foreman.

In spite of threats, bombings and murder, the election took place on the announced date, November 3, 1958. Had it not been for acts of violence that sacrificed men, women and children, voting would have been normal. As it happened, from 72% to 75% of the normal number of voters cast their ballots. Since municipal and local offices were also at stake, there was keen interest in the results.

In 1958, under these conditions of intimidation and terror, 54.01% of the eligible electorate voted. This compares with a voter turnout of about 60% in recent Presidential elections in the United States.

THE MYTH OF THE 20,000 CORPSES

The real terrorists were those who threw bombs into police stations and crowded streetcars and who murdered candidates for public office in order to destroy all democratic institutions.

However, the Castro propaganda mill cleverly imputed its own crimes to its victims. The forces of law and order became the murderers and sadists. These big lies were shrewdly disseminated by a minority of U.S. publicists who, wittingly or unwittingly, served the Communist cause with unswerving consistency and consummate guile.

A few days after he had seized power, Fidel Castro charged my Government with having killed 20,000 Cubans. Even though this figure was "patently ridiculous—and every informed person in Cuba knew it—the tremendous surge of popular enthusiasm for the new dictator swept over the voices of reason and unquestionably accepted Castro's macabre arithmetic."

There were many commonsense refutations of this audacious lie. In the first days of Castro rule, the refugees from my regime—voluntary expatriates—began to return from the United States. There were less than two thousand of them. "Cuban jails were emptied of political prisoners; and the total liberated did not go beyond several hundred, all in good condition, hale and well-fed."

Moreover, every important leader of the Castro movement, with the single exception of Ernesto (Ché) Guevara had at one time or another been in the hands of the Cuban Police. These former prisoners of Batista were living refutations of the Castro propaganda, imputing atrocities and bestial tortures to my regime. The plain and self-evident fact was that all of these former prisoners were alive, healthy, unmutilated and untortured.

In January 1959, the weekly magazine, *Bohemia,* published a list of the supposed victims of the Batista regime. This magazine was notorious for its fanatical partisanship of Castro and his movement. Despite its unabashed propaganda, it had flourished without hindrance in Batista Cuba. After Castro took power, however, the editors of *Bohemia* were driven into exile because they had the decency to refuse to serve as pliant instruments of Soviet tyranny.

Bohemia's list of victims consisted primarily of saboteurs and terrorists who were killed in gun battles with the authorities or else in immediate and passionate reprisal by soldiers and policemen who were understandably emotional about seeing their friends and comrades blown to bits. The second largest category consisted of innocent bystanders who got killed in these bombings and gun battles.

The most significant thing about the *Bohemia* total, which was generally accepted as accurate at the time, was that it amounted to slightly over 900 people. Not the 20,000 that Castro alleged!

Let me compare the fictitious reign of terror of Batista with the real reign of terror of Fidel Castro. The figures are those compiled by Carlos Todd.

Some 10,717 people had been killed by Castro and his Communists up to June 1, 1963 as follows:

Executed by order of "Revolutionary Tribunals"	2,897
Executed without any trial whatsoever	4,245
Killed in action against Castro forces	2,962
Missing	613
TOTAL	10,717

By comparison, during the seven years of my second Administration, there were no legal executions (because we had no death sentence) and the number of Castro supporters and bystanders killed otherwise is estimated by the hostile source, *Bohemia,* at about 900.

Todd estimated that 965,000 people (over 14% of the Cuban population) had been arrested for political reasons at one time or another and that 81,706 persons were in prisons, of whom 16,120 were in concentration camps and 2,146 in G–2 torture farms.

Over 6.6% of Cuba's population, 449,450 persons, left the island since Castro took power. Of these, 2,742 left secretly in small boats and it is estimated that over 600 more were killed in the attempt.

Of these refugees, 385,000 were in the United States, 42,000 in Latin America, 21,000 in Europe and 1,450 scattered elsewhere. An additional 3,401 gained asylum in foreign embassies. Of these, 3,165 were given safe conduct out of the country, leaving 236 still in the embassies. Castro agents frequently violated the right of asylum, entered the embassies by force and murdered the refugees.

Some 230,000 Cubans on the Island had passports and visa waivers, but could not get transport. Another 385,000 applied for passports and visas. Thus, a conservative estimate would be that 1,067,000 Cubans—almost a sixth of the total population—had left the country or were seeking to leave it.

These figures are necessarily incomplete and understatements because not all the executions, murders, imprisonments and shipments to concentration camps are known. Moreover, the processes at work are continuous. The mills of death continue to grind throughout Cuba.

Earl E. T. Smith

CONSPIRACY IN "FOGGY BOTTOM"

Batista's sudden departure from Havana on January 1, 1959, and Castro's dramatic accession to power convinced many Americans that, somehow, American policy was to blame. Smith, who served as ambassador to Cuba in the last days of the Batista government, later condemned elements in American society, particularly a liberal press and the State Department, for their part in publicizing Castro's revolution.

THE day-by-day actions of those on the Fourth Floor of the State Department shaped United States-Latin American foreign policy as far as Cuba was concerned. Stress was laid by these officers on pleasing liberal Latin American opinion, sometimes at the risk of sacrificing American self-respect.

I will list some of the day-by-day actions of those on the Fourth Floor of the State Department who shaped American foreign policy toward Cuba (not listed in order of importance):

1. Suspending the sale of arms and ammunition to the government of Cuba, which had a devastating psychological effect upon those supporting the government of Cuba. In the reverse, the action gave a great psychological uplift to the Castro followers. It forced Batista to turn to other sources for arms, entailing much delay. Also, the United States' refusal made it

Condensed from *The Fourth Floor* by Earl E. T. Smith, pp. 115–136. © Copyright 1962 by Earl E. T. Smith. Reprinted by permission of Random House, Inc.

difficult for Cuba to obtain arms from other nations.

2. Refusal to honor outstanding and prepaid orders for arms.

3. Suspending shipment of all replacement parts for combat equipment.

4. Advising the Department of Defense not to ship controversial military equipment. Such steps were considered a withdrawal of support for the government of Cuba.

5. Not fulfilling our commitment to deliver the twenty armored cars.

6. Not living up to our promise to deliver fifteen training planes.

7. Issuing public statements that hurt the government of Cuba, aided the rebels, and did not help the United States—such as publicizing the news of suspended shipment of the 1,950 Garand rifles; publicizing the news of suspended shipment of Military Defense Assistance Program equipment; publicizing the news that the United States was shipping arms to neither the government of Cuba nor to the rebels. By such actions, the lower echelon of the State Department created the impression in the minds of the public that the United States gave the status of belligerency to the revolutionaries.

8. Intervention by innuendo—persuading other governments not to sell arms to the government of Cuba.

9. Refusing to permit military service officers, attached to the Military Assistance Advisory Groups, to carry out fully their functions as prescribed under the Hemispheric Military Assistance Program; that is, playing down all activities which could be deemed offensive to the revolutionaries.

10. Bringing pressure to bear on the government of Cuba by consistently calling to its attention the violation of the provisions of the Military Defense Assistance Program with Cuba, which stated that the use of military equipment for any other purpose than hemispheric defense must have prior consent of the United States.

11. Bringing pressure to bear on the government of Cuba by stating repeatedly that the infantry battalion, which had been equipped through the Military Defense Assistance Program, was actively engaged in suppressing the rebellion in Oriente Province and then attempting to force the government to break up and retire from active service this infantry battalion.

12. Requesting the government of Cuba to disengage *all* the Military Defense Assistance Program equipped and trained personnel from the combat area.

13. Embarrassing the government of Cuba by delivering a formal note in March 1958 bringing these matters to their attention and requesting a report.

14. Not bringing sufficient pressure to bear on the Justice Department to enforce our neutrality laws.

15. Permitting Dr. Carlos Prío Socarrás and his supporters to violate United States neutrality laws. Dr. Prío was permitted to enter the United States in the spring of 1956 on parole status. If he violated American laws, it was agreed, his parole status was automatically broken. Under the agreement, he could have been removed from the United States. Batista was convinced that Dr. Prío and his agents were the main source of supply of arms, ammunition, and bodies to the Sierra Maestra. Indictment of Dr. Prío was not obtained until the middle of February 1958. Then, he was immediately released on bail. The activities of Dr. Prío were of the greatest concern to President Batista. The President told me on numerous occasions that if the United States would control the activities of Dr. Prío, he would be able to cope with Fidel Castro.

16. Asking the Immigration Department to be lenient on certain Cuban revolutionary exiles by permitting them to prolong their visits in this country.

17. Maintaining friendly contacts with representatives of the revolutionaries, thereby giving sympathetic audience and comfort to those who were openly advocating the overthrow of the government of Cuba.

18. Permitting Castro sympathizers and supporters in the United States to form groups and organizations engaged in fund raising and overt propaganda activities.

19. Embarrassing the government of Cuba by instructing me to obtain assurances that the government of Cuba would not bomb Cuban cities where rebels were situated, with American Military Assistance Program bombers using napalm bombs.

20. Maintaining close contact with Herbert Matthews, of the *New York Times,* who gave the impression by his editorial conduct of advocating Batista's downfall.

The following colloquy took place on September 8, 1960, when William D. Pawley, former United States Ambassador to Peru and to Brazil, testified before a sub-committee of the United States Senate to investigate the "Communist

Threat to the United States Through the Caribbean":

MR. J. G. SOURWINE (CHIEF COUNSEL): Mr. Ambassador, you have made clear to us in your testimony your belief that many policies with respect to Latin America have been made in the State Department not at the top level but at a lower level. As you explained it, they are made on the fourth floor and not on the fifth floor.
Is there any question in your mind that this situation affects the internal security of the United States?
MR. PAWLEY: Yes, I think it has a direct bearing on this nation's security.

On June 12, 1961, Robert C. Hill, former United States Ambassador to Mexico, to Costa Rica and to El Salvador, also former Assistant Secretary of State in charge of Congressional Relations, testified as follows before the sub-committee of the United States Senate to investigate the "Communist Threat to the United States Through the Caribbean":

THE CHAIRMAN (SENATOR [JAMES] EASTLAND): Now you state all the intelligence from the CIA and other agencies in 1957 and 1958 before Castro grabbed power in Cuba indicated that he was pro-Communist?
MR. HILL: I don't say all the intelligence did, Senator Eastland, but, as I said earlier, Castro and his affiliations were brought to my attention by intelligence representatives of the United States that were assigned to Mexico. They started talking to me about Castro and the problem early in 1957. I was very busy getting started in Mexico as the Ambassador and much of 1957 went by before I could review the developments in Cuba regarding Mr. Castro. The intelligence reports from our Embassy in 1958 started to pick up—and 1959—showing more and more indications of Communism, pro-Communism—and Communists that were surrounding Fidel Castro in Cuba.
THE CHAIRMAN: That is correct. It picked up before he assumed power in 1959, the reports that he was pro-Communist and surrounded by Communists.
Now the question I am going to ask you is this: wasn't it your judgment that the Caribbean desk of the State Department of the United States was pro-Castro?
MR. HILL: Before I went to Mexico?
THE CHAIRMAN: Sir?
MR. HILL: I recall the fact that in the spring of 1957 Earl Smith, who went to Cuba as the Ambassador, came to my office and asked me to talk with him about his preparations for his Cuban assignment.
I had known Ambassador Smith at the Republican conventions held in Chicago and San Francisco. I actually worked with him in 1956 in San Francisco on foreign policy matters.
I said, "Earl, I am sorry that you are going to Cuba. You might be interested to know that 'Chip' Bohlen was supposed to go to Cuba." This sort of set him back. He said, "What do you mean, that Ambassador Bohlen was going to be transferred from Moscow to Havana?" I said "That was the plan a few months ago. Then the President and Secretary Dulles decided to send him to Manila. You are assigned to Cuba to preside over the downfall of Batista. The decision has been made that Batista has to go. You must be very careful."
THE CHAIRMAN: The decision was made where?
MR. HILL: I am talking about the corridors of the State Department, Senator.
THE CHAIRMAN: But it was your judgment that the decision had been made by the State Department that Batista had to go?
MR. HILL: I am not saying the decision at the top, but the decision down at the lower level.
THE CHAIRMAN: I asked you about the Caribbean Section.
MR. HILL: It was common knowledge in the Department of State that Batista had to go. I told Ambassador Smith this.
THE CHAIRMAN: That Castro would come into power?
MR. HILL: That is correct. I told Ambassador Smith that he should request from the Secretary of State to take men that he had confidence in, to Havana with him, including his Minister because if he was not careful, his reputation would be destroyed. I recall that we had lunch at the Chevy Chase Club along with my wife. At that time he asked me if I had any suggestions as to who might be available for the Minister's job at the Embassy in Havana. I gave him the names of Foreign Service officers that I felt could be helpful and had a knowledge of the area. None of them would accept the job. Some of the men told me privately, "I don't want to go to Havana because Castro is coming into power." They told me that there is going to be grave trouble down there. They said they had young children and did not want to become involved.

I further told Ambassador Smith not to leave the Embassy. I said, "You stay in the vicinity of your residence in the chancery until you know what is going on in Havana. Don't travel outside the area of the capital." I tried to be as helpful to him as possible.

My predecessor as United States Ambassador to Cuba, Arthur Gardner, testified on August 27, 1960, before the same sub-committee of the United States Senate that "for two years the United States was gradually making Batista feel we were pulling the rug out from under him," and that he (Gardner) had been ignored, overlooked and circumvented by the State Department.

* * *

In addition to the harassing activities against American citizens, American property owners, and the Yateras water plant, American firms suffered huge losses due to sabotage, plundering, and confiscation. American Marines, sailors, and citizens were kidnaped. Cuban commercial aircraft with Americans aboard were hijacked. There were depredations against the United States government-owned $100,000,000 Nicaro Nickel properties. The revolutionaries had utter disregard for American lives and property.

Nevertheless, the liberal press and the Fourth Floor of the State Department continued to sympathize with the revolutionaries.

The Embassy in Havana maintained normal relations with the recognized, friendly government of Cuba. The Fourth Floor maintained relations with the representatives of the revolutionaries and gave sympathetic attention to their requests. Not only were rebel spokesmen cordially received, at times the Latin American corridors were filled with partisans of the Cuban revolution.

During all this period the United States gave asylum to all Cuban exiles. Many Cuban exiles were openly violating the neutrality laws and the criminal code of the United States through exportation of arms, ammunition, and bodies to the revolutionaries; by the launching of armed expeditions from Florida shores; and by giving training in demolition and sabotage to Castro volunteers. The worst offender was Dr. Carlos Prío Socarrás and his agents.

The revolutionaries openly boasted that only about 10 percent of arms exported from the United States to Cuba was apprehended by the United States authorities. Arms and bodies were smuggled out of the United States by aircraft and boats to Fidel Castro in the Sierra Maestra and to Raúl Castro in the Sierra Cristal.

The harassing activities on the part of the revolutionaries against American property and against American citizens took place not only in Cuba but also in Miami. On April 4 President Batista complained that a large group of members of the 26th of July Movement were molesting Cuban pilots of Cubana Airways at the Miami Airport. Three Cuban pilots had received physical harm. The objective of the revolutionaries in Miami was to stop commercial planes from flying between Miami and Havana in accordance with their schedules.

I informed Assistant Secretary [Roy] Rubottom of the President's complaint. He immediately contacted the Justice Department and also notified the two Florida Senators, [George] Smathers and [Spessard] Holland. As a result, Cubana Airways was able to resume their scheduled flights.

The State Department notified the Embassy that shipments of non-combat equipment to the government of Cuba had been approved. However, it would not approve the shipment of replacement parts for combat equipment. The State Department, therefore, had decided not only to suspend the shipment of arms to Cuba, but also to suspend the shipment of all replacement parts for combat equipment.

In early April many members of the American press descended upon the city of Santiago—the headquarters of the revolutionaries—in anticipation of the general strike, and sensing that Santiago would be a better source of news than Havana.

On April 8 seven Americans were arrested in Santiago. They were representatives of the American press and American broadcasting stations. The reason given by Prime Minister Guell for their arrest was that the government of Cuba was worried about their safety. The position of the government was that if one was killed by the revolutionaries, it would be blamed on the government and it would be most embarrassing. The government was trying to discourage members of the press from going into rebel territory. Due to the efforts of Minister Counselor Braddock, First Secretary Topping, and myself we were able to obtain the release by two o'clock in the morning of all these gentlemen.

There were no Embassies of Communist countries in Cuba during Batista's Presidency. He forced the Soviet Embassy to close and took steps which brought about Russia's severance of diplomatic relations with Cuba. These steps occurred before I was appointed United States Ambassador to Cuba.

Under Batista the Bureau for Repression of Communist Activities, known as BRAC, was set up. This agency, with American aid, was in operation for years. At times, it was effective. At other times, I found it necessary to appeal for more vigorous action.

Although we had much and consistent intangible evidence of the Communist infiltration and control of the 26th of July Movement, the Communists were too smart to give us any one piece of all-conclusive and irrefutable evidence of their control of the Castro movement. Many times, I had asked President Batista and Prime Minister Guell to give me their proof with which I could further substantiate my charges to the Department that the Castro revolution was not only infiltrated, but also under the control of the Communists.

In early April, I received word from Dr. Guell that he had additional evidence to substantiate the connection between the Communists and the Castro movement. The Bureau for the Repression of Communist Activities, in connection with the police, had raided the headquarters of the Communist newspaper, Hoy, and had found, according to Dr. Guell, propaganda literature of the 26th of July Movement which had been printed on the same press used by the newspaper Hoy.

I instructed the Embassy press officer, Mr. John Williams, to investigate and report to me on the charges. From the evidence that existed, it appeared that the 26th of July propaganda literature had been turned out by the press of the Communist paper, Hoy.

Mr. Bruce Henderson of Time-Life was quite indignant that I should have sent the Embassy public relations officer to attend a press conference held by the Cuban police in which the government of Cuba presented alleged proof tying up Fidel Castro with the Communists. It was his opinion, shared by some other members of the American press, that the Cuban police had just put on a show to pin the Communist label on Castro.

Mr. Henderson was considered one of the top Latin American reporters for Time, Inc. It happened that, late that day, my wife, Florence, met him at a reception. She found Mr. Henderson to be charming and invited him to the residence for a swim and lunch—not knowing of our contretemps. We talked for hours on the Cuban situation. Although Mr. Henderson had preconceived ideas, approaching antagonism to me, he did understand my position. I promised to keep him as fully informed as permitted on political developments; we parted, I believe, sharing a feeling of mutual respect.

On the night of April 8 I received a visit at the Embassy residence from the Papal Nuncio, Monsignor Luigi Centoz and the Bishop of Havana, Monsignor Alfredo Muller. Bishop Muller was on his way to Oriente to pick up Archbishop Perez Serantes to go up in the hills by helicopter to visit Castro to obtain a truce.

The Papal Nuncio said that because of my great interest in obtaining a truce would I assist them in mediating. I was only authorized to reaffirm the position of non-intervention of the United States and so I told them I had no authority to mediate or to take part in the preliminary demarche. If the Church were able to establish a truce, I was sure that the United States State Department would make some sort of statement showing its desire for a peaceful solution of the troublesome days in Cuba. More than that I was not authorized to promise.

The Papal Nuncio asked if the Navy would supply a helicopter to transport Archbishop Serantes and Monsignor Muller to the hills. Such a flight, I said, would create a lot of publicity and advised the Papal Nuncio against the action at that time. Then I suggested that the timing might be more propitious if they were to postpone their visit to Castro until a later date.

The proposed visit by the Church dignitaries had been cleared with President Batista ten days before when his position was a little precarious. In the next ten days Batista's position was much stronger. Therefore, I suggested that it might be prudent to clear again the visit with the President. I also had information that the general strike would take place momentarily. Any overtures for a truce would be more effective at a later date. A visit in the hills in a helicopter would attract quite a good deal of attention. It would be propitious for the Church to make sure that their expedition be successful; if unsuccessful, such a visit could place the Church in an embarrassing light.

The next morning I was thankful for the advice I had given the Papal Nuncio, because the much anticipated general strike was called on the morning of April 9.

By eleven o'clock conditions were still normal in Havana. News from the outlying provinces was different. In Oriente where the strike did not start until the afternoon, it was more or less effective. However, the real test would come in Havana. If the strike was not effective in this great city it would be broken in the rest of the island.

The strike in Havana was not effective because the student group's committee had decided not to co-operate with the 26th of July Movement. If Castro had been willing to let the Directório

Revolucionário name the Mayor and other officials in the city, they would have actively co-operated and the results might have been different. Also there was no confidence on the part of the general public in Castro, and Batista had the support of the Army, police force, and labor leaders.

At 11:00 A.M. I received a telephone call from Mr. William Wieland, Director, MID, Department of State. The conversation began as follows:

Wieland: "How are things down there this morning?"

Ambassador: "Nice and quiet—the war is still being fought in the United States."

I knew the Director of MID and others in his section were hopefully expecting the general strike to be a success, and it pleased me to be able to report otherwise.

The general strike in Havana was completely ineffective and only lasted for a short while, much to the disappointment of many influential persons in the United States. There was some disruption, but Havana was back to normal in a few hours.

The rebels had boasted that 50,000 Cubans would go on strike in Havana and they were sickened by their complete failure.

At this moment, after the failure of the general strike, Batista apparently felt that he was in the ascendancy. He decided to step up the military campaign. The Fourth Floor, however, held that a resumption of strong-arm methods would not create a climate for peace. The Fourth Floor further maintained that strong-arm methods only meant fighting terror with terror, which would further turn public opinion against Batista. For Batista to seek a purely military solution was unfortunate.

The State Department instructed me to express to Batista and government officials our hope that conditions for acceptable elections would be instituted, such as: restoration of constitutional guarantees and lifting of the press censorship; invitations to OAS, the world press and UN observers to witness the elections. Batista promised to comply with every one of these suggestions and gave me his word that the elections would be honest.

*   *   *

The general strike was a complete failure because economic conditions were good; there was no co-ordination on the part of the revolutionaries in Havana; there was no confidence on the part of the general public in Castro outside of Oriente Province; the government of Cuba retained the full support of the armed services, the police force and the labor leaders.

The collapse of the much touted strike was a severe psychological blow to the Castro forces. Had the Department been willing this would have been an opportune time for the United States to apply pressure on Batista to make overtures for peace, to include his complete retirement from the political picture. The Cuban Episcopacy was prepared to approach Batista with concrete suggestions and sought the support of the United States. The State Department would back no solution. Yet the Department well realized that, because of our dominant position in Cuba, no solution could be successful unless fully supported by the United States.

Rebel spokesmen in Washington were pressuring the State Department to try to obtain spiritual aid to embarrass the Batista government. These partisans of the rebel cause were attempting to convince the State Department that the government of Cuba was bombing Cuban cities, where rebels were situated, with American Military Assistance Program bombers.

The State Department was told by the representatives of the revolutionaries that the rebels would try to capture some cities and the government of Cuba would use MAP-supplied bombers to drop napalm bombs obtained from the Dominican Republic. I was instructed to obtain assurances from the proper authorities that the government of Cuba would not take any of these actions.

With the advance knowledge and consent of Foreign Minister Guell, my secretary recorded his remarks made over the telephone:

We never bomb any city or any large town. There is not the remotest possibility of any such occurrence. My government is extremely sorry to receive this kind of inquiry because it does not adjust to the real facts. There is no chance of the revolutionaries capturing any of these cities. What they do sometimes is to make a hit and run raid on a small place. We never bomb any city. I repeat, there is not the remotest possibility that we would do anything like that. We haven't even done this in the Sierra because of the farms surrounding the place. Even in combat we manage as much as possible so as not to cause many deaths. We try to capture prisoners, while the rebels shoot our soldiers when they engage in action. We have purchased arms some place else and we have paid for these arms.

At this time the Department issued a public statement saying that it was shipping arms to neither the rebels nor to the government of Cuba; by this statement the State Department created the impression that the United States considered the rebels as being on the same plane as the government of Cuba.

I pointed out in a cable to the State Department that we had given indirect aid to the rebels by not fulfilling our commitment to deliver the twenty armored cars and by publicizing the suspension of arms. I strongly recommended that we cease issuing public statements that would hurt the government of Cuba, aid the rebels, and not help the alleged impartial position of the United States.

On April 12 I wrote a memorandum for my personal records in longhand to the effect that we were receiving more and more reports indicating that the Communist Party of Cuba (Partido Socialista Popular) was supporting the 26th of July Movement. The latest reports were from J. Edgar Hoover.

The prestige of the Castro forces had shrunk because of the failure of the general strike. As a result, the revolutionaries believed some drama was necessary to regain the spotlight.

On April 15 the Embassy learned from a reliable source in the International Co-operation Administration (Point

Four Program) that the Castro forces were going to kidnap the American Ambassador. Because of loss of prestige, as the result of the failure of the general strike, the 26th of July Movement wished to regain the limelight through some publicity stunt. It later developed that they dropped the idea to kidnap me. Instead the forces of Raúl Castro planned wholesale kidnaping of Americans, including Marines and sailors.

In the meantime, the efforts to obtain a truce on the part of the Church were continuing. Bishop Alfredo Muller of Havana and Bishop Alberto Martin Villaverde of the Province of Matanzas sent word to Castro asking for an emissary to discuss a peaceful solution.

Amongst the endeavors for a peaceful solution proposed by Church dignitaries were: that the Cuban Episcopacy, interpreting the thought and sentiments of the majority of the Cuban people, believed it to be incumbent upon themselves to halt violence under which the political problems of the country were being debated. The Church did not believe that peace in the land, with the restoration of democratic rights, could be obtained through violence and bloodshed.

The Cuban Episcopacy stated that they would endeavor to obtain the following objectives:

(A) Maintenance of public order.
(B) Respect for the fundamental rights of citizens.
(C) Free electoral process with equal rights and guarantees for all political parties.

These objectives could be obtained through the formation of a broadly-based neutral government, whose members would not be permitted to run for elective office in the ensuing elections. Its constitution would be drawn up according to the Constitution of 1940 and it would hold powers in conformity with Articles 281 and 282 of that Constitution.

Under this plan the Episcopacy would assume the responsibility of proposing the person to be designated as Prime Minister of the Cabinet. The Episcopacy would recommend persons for the Cabinet but the selection of the Cabinet would be the responsibility of the Prime Minister. The Episcopacy was prepared to enlist the support of social and civic groups.

In an effort to co-ordinate all national opinion on the political conflict church dignitaries were prepared to visit the President of the Republic to notify him of the endeavors to be realized. The Church was prepared to notify the Castros of their endeavors and also prepared to notify the leading representatives of the revolution in the United States.

From the Castros and from the representatives of the revolutionaries in the United States the Episcopacy would try to obtain written expressions, in the shortest period of time, of the proposals believed by each of them to be necessary to arrive at a peaceful solution to the national quarrel.

Once the opinions requested were obtained, the Episcopacy would incorporate them where compatible with a formula for the restoration of peace with democratic rights.

The Church was prepared to carry the ball by itself, but even the Cuban Episcopacy could not bring about a peaceful solution without the support of the United States. (The efforts of the Church by itself were not sufficient, as the Church carried less weight in Cuba than in other Latin American countries.) The Department was not willing actively to support any propositions for a peaceful solution. The reason given was that any such active support would be considered as intervening in the internal affairs of Cuba. Actually, we were consistently intervening in our day-to-day actions to bring about the downfall of the Batista dictatorship and to turn the government of Cuba over to Fidel Castro.

Before the United States Senate Sub-Committee to Investigate the Communist Threat Through the Caribbean I testified as follows on August 30, 1960:

Because Batista was the dictator who unlawfully seized power, American people assumed Castro must, on the other hand, represent liberty and democracy. The crusader role which the press and radio bestowed on the bearded rebel blinded the people to the leftwing political philosophy with which even at that time he was already on record. [Castro's] speeches as a student leader, his interviews as an exile while in Mexico, Costa Rica, and elsewhere clearly outlined a Marxist trend of political thought. The official United States attitude toward Castro could not help but be influenced by the pro-Castro press and radio; certain members of Congress picked up the torch for him.

In response to a question from Senator Eastland regarding who was principally responsible for Castro's rise to power, my testimony went on as follows:

Mr. Smith: Without the United States, Castro would not be in power today. I will put it as straight as that to you, sir.
Senator [Roman] Hruska: But the responsibility for that is a composite thing?
Mr. Smith: [It] is a composite, that is correct.
Senator Hruska: There may have been certain quarters in which there were more virulent advocates than others, but, just the same, it is a composite thing. Without that composite nature, very likely, the result which did follow may not have happened.
Mr. Smith: That is correct. In other words, I do not think it is fair to say that this individual or that individual or that particular agency, in itself, per se, is responsible for Castro coming to power. It is the composite.
Senator Eastland: The composite of the United States Government, is that it, and its branches?
Mr. Smith: Composite of those elements that formed the United States Government.
Senator Eastland: That formed the United States Government.
Mr. Smith: I mentioned segments of the press, certain members of Congress, the CIA, the State Department. All of them took a hand in this, Senator.
Senator [Thomas] Dodd: But in any composite picture, I think we all recognize that there are some influences that are

stronger than others. They are never all the same.
Mr. Smith: No. Some must share a greater part of the guilt than others.
Senator Dodd: And some can do more than others.
Mr. Smith: And some are in a position to do much more.
Senator Dodd: That is what I think we are driving at.
Senator Eastland: And the agencies of the United States Government could do, of course, more than members of Congress or the press or anyone else.
Mr. Smith: That is true. You have all sorts of agencies.
Senator Dodd: Certainly, you can say it the other way. You can say that without the United States Government, the other factors of the composite picture could not do anything. If the government had stood firm and said, "We will not assist Castro," the fact that there were many other elements of our society who were sympathetic to him could not have brought it about, isn't that true?
Senator Hruska: Conversely, if the other elements—and I take what we would consider exterior elements; let's take business and the press—for example, had the press, in its opinion-making power, been antagonistic toward Castro, no amount of formal governmental action could have overcome that massive factor.
Mr. Smith: That is true.
Senator Hruska: The same thing is true with reference to implementing Castro. If and when business located and having investments in Cuba would either by blackmail or by so-called taxes support financially the Castro movement, that was something which, likewise, would be very helpful to those who in formal government circles would say, "Let us also help Castro."
Mr. Smith: Those who paid tribute at the end were doing it for their own self-protection because they felt that if they did not do it they were going to lose their holdings.
Senator Eastland: As a matter of fact, now, wasn't it the impartiality of the United States Government that brought Castro to power?
Mr. Smith: Wasn't it the impartiality?
Senator Eastland: Yes.
Mr. Smith: Senator, we are responsible for bringing Castro in power. I do not care how you want to word it.

C. Wright Mills

LISTEN, YANKEE

A well-known sociologist, C. Wright Mills was noted for his provocative analyses of American society and politics. This vigorous defense of Castro's revolution appeared *before* the Bay of Pigs and the Missile Crisis.

I

LATIN America is enormously rich—in soil, timber, oil, all the metals, the chemicals; it is rich in virtually everything men need to live well. Yet in this plundered continent there exist today some of the most hopelessly impoverished and most consistently exploited people in the world.

Most of these countries—like the old Cuba—are one-crop economies, and thus dependent upon the fluctuations of world prices and the impersonal calculations of foreign bankers.

Most of these countries—like the old Cuba—are, in fact, run by an alliance of foreign capital and local interests of the most retrograde character it is possible to imagine. Most of their governments—like the old Cuba's—are a world joke on the meaning of "constitutional democracy." In this part of the world, governments tend to be branches of private enterprise; "democracy" in much of Latin America is largely a façade tolerated by an army, a ceremony displayed on due occasion.

In many of these countries—like the old Cuba—no real reforms can be undertaken without the approval of The Military, whose take of the national budgets runs well above 20%. Only in Mexico in 1914, in Bolivia in 1952, and in Cuba in 1958–59, have regular armies been smashed by revolution; and *only* in these three countries has there been any attempt really to deal with the basic problems of land.

There is, of course, considerable variety; each country has its own problems as well as those peculiar to this world region. Brazil, for example, has for four years been undergoing a capitalist boom. It is a "dual society": there is the capitalist-rich São Paulo area, with its urban population caught in an inflationary wage-price squeeze; and there is the rest, an internal colony. Perhaps half the population is not in any money economy at all; and in the impoverished northeast, at times, people live off cactus. Brazil is in itself a continent—and a curiously colonial power.

In the six "republics" of Central America, a few hundred elite families own most of the land; a middle class scarcely exists; the immense majority live in drudgery, poverty, sloth; more than half are illiterate. Bananas in Honduras and Panama; cotton in Nicaragua; coffee and bananas in Costa Rica; in the others, coffee—these are the "dessert" export crops around which these economies revolve.

Argentina continues to do nothing of significance to develop its real wealth—land, cattle, grain; three fourths of her people live in the cities, most of them underemployed; industry is stagnant, inflation is continuing, the Government is more and more dependent upon the army. Meanwhile armed men are in the pampas—the finest farmland in Latin America; police terror is frequent in the cities.

Chile, officially embracing the cherished principles of political democracy and free-enterprise capitalism, is getting into hock to financial agencies dominated by the United States. These agencies provide small loans and in return dictate financial policies to a conservative government. One fourth of the population is an inflated white-collar throng. And again, there is utter neglect of the land: Some 86% of it is held in large *fundos,* the owners of which are more interested in profitable speculation in land than in farming it. In Chile, the farming is bad; in Chile, traditional poverty is institutionalized; in Chile, some one third of the men are drunk every week end—and perhaps 60% of the lower classes.

Probably three fourths of the inhabitants of Peru exist outside any money economy, waiting hopelessly on the edge of starvation (average daily caloric intake: 1,900). Sulphur fumes from the copper smelters blanket the wet mountains; the mining towns are not habitations for human beings, but human beings do exist there. And Peru, we are assured, is a highly constitutional democracy.

The recent history of Venezuela is one of economic madness. Professor Edwin Lieuwen states that when the dictator [Juan Vicente] Gomez died in 1935, "an economic dictator had already inherited Venezuela . . . the petroleum industry was the new ruler. The new tyrant was immortal, and political upheavals disturbed it little. It answered only to the demands of the market in the United States and in western Europe and waited for the signals to be called from abroad." Oil accounts for over 90% of Venezuela's foreign income, provides 63% of her Government revenues, but employs only 3% of her labor force. So far as industrial development is concerned, the petroleum industry has led to what the Mexican economist Edmundo Flores calls "a chromeplated dead-end." The constitutionally elected president, [Rómulo] Betancourt, has today inherited the consequences of this economic madness which, according to Paul Johnson, includes: "the highest cost economy in the world, which is driving Venezuelan oil out of the world market; seven dif-

ferent police forces; a huge, over-paid bureaucracy; inflated armed forces equipped with expensive gadgets like supersonic fighters [a nuclear submarine is on order] and a great sheaf of unpaid bills." In the meantime, President Betancourt has been "forced to turn to the U.S. for loans, with all that this entails in social and economic stagnation. Basic land reform has been shelved . . . unemployment is swelling. The growing anger of the mob [of the unemployed of Caracas] can be balanced only by more concessions to the army."

And Mexico? Her great revolution of 1910 and the following years has stalled. In a word, a revolution that began with the demand for land and for liberty seems to be ending in a plutocracy sitting within their state and on top of a capitalist economy—and full of revolutionary rhetoric. The old revolutionaries have become enriched political capitalists. To them, as well as to the newly made middle classes, "revolution" has been and is a highly profitable business —in recent years, 1% of the population has gotten as much as 51% of the national income—yet the governing classes all talk ultra-Left.

The Mexican revolutionaries have long memories: They know that "tourism" alone contributes almost one fourth of their country's foreign-exchange earnings, yet they do not forget that a hundred years ago the United States took by force an enormous chunk of Mexico's national territory. They know well that there is no progressive tax on personal income—but also they remember all about their fight with the United States, only yesterday, when they took their own oil resources into their own hands. They may be old and rich— but they know all about the use of Catholicism in counterrevolutions.

Nowadays, in Mexico, students are demonstrating—against the Yankee; and unlike the United States, Mexico is not monolithic on the question of Cuba. Mexico is split. Even the old revolutionaries see in Fidel Castro something of their own lost youth. The wind that once swept Mexico may yet sweep it again. Despite everything, which today is quite a lot, Mexico is a windy place.

Latin America is a great world region; it is a continent, long and repeatedly plundered; and it is in revolutionary ferment. That it is now in such ferment is a heartening testimony to the will of man not to remain forever an exploited object. For over a century Latin American man has been largely outside world history—except as an object; now he is entering that history—as a subject, with vengeance, with pride, with violence. The unilateral Monroe Doctrine is part of the epoch of Latin American isolation: it is isolationism on a hemispheric scale, and a shield for U.S. exploitation. That epoch, and with it the Monroe Doctrine, is now coming to an end.

But isn't there another side to it? Of course. Latin America *is* a continent, and as such it is various. Convictions about it are as sharply divided as they are passionately held. But insofar as it is possible to describe the general scene in brief, we must pay attention to:

The unbelievable poverty (perhaps two thirds of these people are undernourished); the ill-health (about one half of these people have infectious or deficiency diseases); the illiteracy (about one half); the internal colonies (some one third of these people are outside the Latin American economic and cultural community); the steady exploitation (two thirds of these people are in semifeudal conditions of work); the one-crop export economies (and so the perilous dependence upon the fluctuations of foreign markets); the unjust and inefficient systems of land ownership and tenure (two thirds of the land is controlled—and often misused—by native oligarchies and foreign corporations); the foreign domination (perhaps a majority of the "extractive industries" is owned or controlled by foreign capital); the inadequate transportation systems (what exist are mainly means of transporting raw materials from inland to coast, rather than means suitable for the development of internal markets); the ineffective credit systems and the lack of any real trade within and between these countries themselves (trade between them runs to about 7% of the world trade of Latin America); the repeated interventions—commercial and military—by great world powers; the political domination by feudal oligarchies, mixed with foreign corporate interests, and subject to the arbitrary actions of inflated armies: The Military Arbiters. (Since the end of the Second World War, governments of Latin America have "changed hands" without regard to "formal procedures" at least 31 times.)

Such are the salient realities of Latin America—yesterday and today.

Yesterday—but not today—they were the realities of Cuba.

II

The second general fact it is necessary to understand is the role the United States has played and is playing inside Latin America. This role I have already indicated: the "foreign capital" involved is largely U.S. capital; the aid given to the local armies, and hence in support of the feudal oligarchies, is U.S. aid. Inside Latin America, the U.S. Government has supported reactionary circles and do-nothing ruling strata. Its role has generally been and continues to be that of stabilizing their domination and so the continued sloth. Its aid has been largely to give *them* arms and other military support, in the name of "Hemispheric Defense," which has meant defense against their own people.

About this "aid": Since the end of World War II, the U.S. has given in direct aid about 31 *billion* dollars to countries outside Latin America, and only some 625 *million* dollars to Latin America—less than to the Philippines alone. For its "loans" (which have amounted to some 2.5 billion), the U.S. exacts acceptance of economic policies which, given the declining prices of Latin American commodities, cancel out all aid and loans. "During the last ten years," Paul Johnson sums it up, "the collapse of world commodity prices (from which the U.S. along with the other advanced industrial countries, has drawn immense benefit) has meant a net reduction in the income of Latin-America of over 1,000 million a year—three times as much, in aggregate, as the sum total of aid and loans the area has received during the same period. This is the brutal arithmetic which explains why tens, perhaps hundreds, of millions of Latin-Americans, poor as they are, are getting steadily poorer."

"Preachments," A. A. Berle Jr. recently remarked, "about the value of private enterprise and investment and the usefulness of foreign capital were, to most students of the situation, a little silly. . . . Probably if the truth were known, this form of economic development in Latin America at the moment is a minority rather than a majority function. . . . Foreign aid or private investment may industrialize, may increase production, and still leave the masses in as bad shape as ever."

U.S. trade with Latin America is, of course, larger than U.S. trade with any other world region; U.S. investment in Latin America, amounting now to about 9 billion dollars, is larger than U.S. investment in any other region of the world. Mining properties and oil are the largest elements in this investment, and both are needed by the U.S. economy as it is now operated. Accordingly: the job of the U.S. Government has been to promote trade and to protect investment. In pursuance of these aims, the official line has been to maintain political stability among the dominated, irrespective forms of government, in order that business might continue as usual. The rest is oratorical embellishment—perhaps needed to insure the votes of these governments in the U.N. That, in a few sentences, seems to me the essential truth of the matter.

But there is more to it: The U.S. has supplied arms to all 20 of these countries, and to 12 of them has made grants of military aid; it has set up Military Missions, which, in the opinion of Professor Lieuwen—author of the most balanced and comprehensive account of the matter—have "no genuine military objective." The official rationale given for all this is fear of Communist aggression. But: In any real East-West fight, the kind of arms provided seem quite irrelevant; and the Communist parties inside Latin America are not only generally weak but clearly grow on the deplorable economic and social conditions which these U.S. policies help to insure. Regardless of the sincerity of official intentions, the real functions of such military aid have been persuasively stated by Professor Lieuwen: In most of these countries the armed forces "play key political roles" and are "seemingly insatiable" in their desire for arms. "Thus military training and assistance are provided to secure—and to insure—political cooperation. . . . Political gains [to the U.S.] are expected to flow from the military programs: well-disposed governments, support for U.S. policies in international organizations, and assurance of access to military bases and strategic raw materials in Latin America. A further objective of the military programs is to promote political stability in this low-priority area so that our maximum energies can be devoted elsewhere. The simple reasoning is that the better the army in any Latin American republic, the less likely that internal order will be subverted."

That more democratic *forms* of government have come about in several Latin American countries since the end of World War II—Mr. A. A. Berle Jr. states—has "been treated by the Department of State as an almost trivial change—and not a wholly agreeable one." (Perhaps the Department has been sound in its judgment of the triviality of the change.) Mr. Berle adds that in the past, the State Department has carried on its friendship with "dictators" who have had "to maintain a steady and frequently an increasingly cruel policy of suppressing popular opposition by police methods [but] the United States took pains not to show sympathy with their opponents—irrespective of the quality of the men or of the forces they symbolized. In this attitude, the Department was supported by a steady stream of reports from the chiefs of dictatorial secret police to the effect that all their opponents were 'Communist.' This material found its way into the State Department files, and was fed to Congressional and other officials. It proved a useful excuse for harrying and harassing entirely genuine democratic leaders and movements. . . . Whether in their own countries, or in exile or refuge in the United States, the democratic leaders found themselves baffled, discredited, almost persecuted by the Government of the United States—supposedly the symbol of democracy."

Is it any wonder, then, that in the minds of many intelligent Latin Americans, the United States of America more often than not stands for political tyranny, economic exploitation, continued impoverishment, and military domination? Is it any wonder that Mr. Nixon was spit upon during his attempt to make a good-will tour? That it was a surprise to most North Americans reveals the inadequacy of the North American press: It was a reflection of everyday realities in Latin America.

"The sad truth," write Professors Pike and Bray, "is that the state of affairs in Latin America has sunk to the level that the United States could help to destroy a democratic regime by 'embracing' it." In one respect at least, the United States in the 20th century stands in the same relationship to Latin America as Czarist Russia in the 19th century stood to Europe: The U.S.A. is a reactionary menace to any real attempt to modify the basic realities of Latin America. Generally, whenever in Latin America people have really begun to get on the move, in the face of their movement the policies and the lack of policies of the United States have been consistently counterrevolutionary.

Certainly that has been and certainly that is the case in connection with the revolution in Cuba.

III

In the general context of Latin America and in terms of the role in Latin America of the United States, the Cuban revolution is a new phenomenon. Some of its features have been available elsewhere, at one time or another, but the specific Cuban combination is historically unique.

1: Like Mexico's revolution of 40 years ago, Cuba's is based upon the peasantry, but the land reform in Cuba is far more thorough, rapid, and successful than Mexico's or Bolivia's. (In many recent years, Mexico has still had to import foodstuffs.) Elsewhere, there is no significant land reform.

2: In at least six Latin American nations, the vicious role of the traditional military apparatus in political, social and economic life has been destroyed. In Cuba, this apparatus has been totally and almost suddenly smashed—and with it the dominant economic powers.

3: The Cuban revolution has swiftly destroyed the economic basis of capitalism—both foreign and Cuban. Most of this power was foreign—in fact, North American. It has now been destroyed with a thoroughness unique in Latin American history.

4: Moreover, Cuba's economic success—due primarily to her successful and intelligent agrarian reform, and helped at a decisive juncture by her economic agreements and trading with Soviet-bloc countries—makes Cuba impregnable to effective economic blockade or pressure from U.S. interests.

There are, of course, other features of this revolution, but it is this combination that is unique in Latin America. And it is this combination, with various modifications and additions, that in my judgment is now a major alternative to continued misery elsewhere in Latin America. One thing that might stop it from becoming the most probable alternative is a drastic change in U.S. policy. But given the character of the political economy of the U.S. today, I do not think it reasonable to expect a change of the sort that would be needed: The United States Government would have to actively help Latin Americans destroy the vested interests inside their own countries as well as the vested interests of U.S. corporations now operating in these countries. For it is this alliance of U.S. capital with local interests that now rules much of Latin America today—and so helps to keep it in the condition that it is in.

Without the destruction of these interests—both Latin and North American —no real economic changes can reasonably be expected, certainly not at a sufficiently rapid rate. And without such structural economic changes, "democracy" will remain what it now is in most of this continent: A farce, a fraud, a ceremony.

IV

And that is why I am for the Cuban revolution. I do not worry about it, I worry for it and with it. Like most Cubans, I too believe that this revolution is a moment of truth, and like some Cuban revolutionaries, I too believe that such truth, like all revolutionary truth, is perilous.

Any moment of such military and economic truth *might* become an epoch of political and cultural lies. It *might* harden into any one of several kinds of dictatorial tyranny. But I do not believe that this is at all inevitable in Cuba. And I do believe that should it happen it would be due, in very large part, to the role the Government of the United States has been and is continuing to play in Cuban affairs.

Were I a Cuban, I have no doubt that I would be working with all my effort for the success of my revolution. But I am not a Cuban. I am a Yankee. To me, this does not mean that I am any the less "for" their revolution. For, like L. T. Hobhouse, whose creed at this point, I share, I cannot give unconditional loyalties to any institution, man, state, movement or nation. My loyalties are conditional upon my own convictions and my own values. And in this matter, both of these lie more with the Cuban revolution than with the official United States reaction to it.

The policies the United States has pursued and is pursuing against Cuba are based upon a profound ignorance, and are shot through with hysteria. I believe that if they are continued they will result in more disgrace and more disaster for the image of my country before Cuba, before Latin America, and before the world.

Moreover, I think that U.S. policies and lack of policies are very real factors in *forcing* the Government of Cuba to align itself politically with the Soviet bloc, as against assuming a genuinely neutralist and hence peaceful world orientation. In fact, these policies are making it very difficult indeed for Cubans even to discuss such an orientation. More than any other single factor, these U.S. policies are forcing the Cuban Government to become "harder," to become more restrictive of freedom of expression inside Cuba. In brief, they are forcing Cubans to identify all "minority views" with "counterrevolution." And they are forcing the Cuban Government to identify "anticommunism" with "counterrevolution."

Let me say, as flatly as I am able to say, that were I a Cuban, acting in the Cuban revolution today, I too should feel it necessary to make this latter identification. For the plain truth is that the kind of ignorant and hysterical "anticommunism" that is now the mood, the tone, and the view of many of the highest governmental officials of the United States of America *is* of the McCarthy type. And I am just as opposed to this as I am to Stalinist practice and proclamation. Surely our aim, in the U.S.A. and in the U.S.S.R., should be to go beyond both.

The Cuban Government, as of mid-1960, is *not* "Communist" in any of the senses legitimately given to this word. The Communist Party of Cuba, as a party, does *not* pose any serious threat to Cuba's political future. The leading men of Cuba's Government are not "Communist," or even Communist-type, as I have experienced communism in Latin America and in research work in the Soviet Union. On all these counts, I find the Cuban argument, as presented in letter number five, generally convincing.

It is worth examining the evidence presented by North American writers of the contrary opinion, for to do so, I believe, is to reveal its weakness. In his article in the October 1960 issue of *For-*

eign Affairs, Mr. A. A. Berle Jr. gives three grounds for his identification of "Cuba" with "Communism":

1: "When Batista fell," Mr. Berle writes, "the hard-core Communist cadres found little, if any, choate force to prevent them from taking over."

This *assumes* that these "hard-core Communist cadres" are necessarily efficient, in contrast to the non-Communist revolutionaries who *made* the revolution against, it so happens, Communist-Party opposition; it assumes that such revolutionaries have been incapable of creating or of being a "choate force." I think both assumptions very dubious, and I would ask: "Has Mr. Berle spent as much as one week in any one INRA zone observing what is going on insofar as personnel is concerned?

2: The second ground for his assumption which Mr. Berle gives is that the defectors from the revolution have stated as their reason for defection that the regime is "Communist." Given the context of their defection—the United States—it would surely be unreasonable to expect them to give any other reason. At any rate, I am certainly not willing, as Mr. Berle presumably is, to take the assertions of these men as either knowledgeable or detached evidence on this important historical matter.

3: The only other ground I find in his essay, Mr. Berle puts it this way: "The undeniable fact is that in result its orientation became, in terms of foreign relations as well as in terms of structure, Communist in character."

In terms of foreign relations: Does it make a government Communist if it trades with the Soviet bloc? If so, many countries indeed are suddenly made "Communist." Does it make a government Communist if it feels itself, rightly or wrongly, to be menaced militarily by a non-Communist country, and so accepts the Soviet Union's protection *on condition* that it *is* invaded? There is, to be sure, room for argument on these questions, but their answers may not merely be assumed. Moreover, the "foreign relations" of Cuba are, as yet, by no means frozen, as Mr. Berle generally assumes.

As for "structure," surely one must ask Mr. Berle to be a little more precise. "Communism" in the world today is neither homogeneous nor unchanging. Cuba's economic structure is certainly not Stalinist. Does Mr. Berle refer to Bolshevism in 1920? To Yugoslavia in 1950? To Khrushchev's Russia today? To Mao's China? Well, what *does* Mr. Berle mean by "Communist"?

The Cuban revolutionary *is* a new and distinct type of left-wing thinker and actor. He is neither capitalist nor Communist. He is socialist in a manner, I believe, both practical and humane. And if Cuba is let alone, I believe that Cubans have a good chance to keep the socialist society they are building practical and humane. If Cubans are properly helped—economically, technically and culturally—I believe they would have a *very* good chance.

I do not agree with this black-or-white thinking of Mr. Berle and many others. I agree with Professor Antonio García of Colombia that Latin America need be subservient neither to the U.S.A. nor the U.S.S.R., and that the essence of U.S. policy has been "to fight Communism with merely political and military means"—to which I would add: and with the most inadvisable identification of everything not in line with the capitalist world as "communism." Such an identification makes the formulation of a cogent foreign policy toward the hungry-nation bloc next to impossible.

v

My worries for Cuba—like those of knowledgeable Cuban revolutionaries—have to do, first, with problems of politics. The Government of Cuba is a revolutionary dictatorship of the peasants and workers of Cuba. It is legally arbitrary. It is legitimized by the enthusiastic support of an overwhelming majority of the people of Cuba. Each of these three facts about it must be recognized, as well as that Professors Pike and Bray are surely correct in their statement that "the formalistic shell of the American way of life was exportable to nineteenth-century Latin America. It is not today."

I do not like such dependence upon

one man as exists in Cuba today, nor the virtually absolute power that this one man possesses. Yet I believe it is not enough either to approve or to disapprove this fact about Cuba. That is much too easy; it is also politically fruitless. One must understand the conditions that have made it so, and that are continuing to make it so; for only then can one consider the prospects of its development. . . . I believe that the revolutionary politics of Cuba are part of a phase, and that I and other North Americans should help the Cubans pass *through* it.

Moreover, the character and the actions of the man in question, Fidel Castro, are not irrelevant to the probable outcome. In my judgment, one must take seriously this man's own attempts to shift roles, even in the middle of his necessary action, and his own astute awareness of the need to develop a more systematic relation between a government of law and the people of Cuba. In this, again, he is acting under great difficulties, many of which are due to the policies and the defaults of the Government of the United States.

As for elections in Cuba today: I share the view of every competent observer that in any election the victory of the *Fidelistas* would be overwhelming. But what seems to me more relevant to the question is that no matter how an election were organized, and no matter how it might be supervised by any international agency, such a victory would be quite meaningless. To have meaningful elections it is necessary to have at least two political parties and it would be necessary for these parties to campaign on some range of issues. The only issue in Cuba today is the revolution, conceived by the Cuban Government primarily as economic and educational construction and as the military defense of Cuba's sovereignty. Any party that campaigned in Cuba today against the revolution and against the present Government's management of it would probably be set upon by the majority of the people of Cuba. So I think it must be faced up to: a real election in Cuba today is an impossible and meaningless idea. It could only be made meaningful by deliberately giving institutional form to the counterrevolution, and that today would not be acceptable to the immense majority of the people of Cuba.

The absence of elections signifies the "absence of democracy" only on the formal assumption that the electoral process is at all times and in all places indispensable to democracy. But be that as it may, an election in Cuba is at the present time an impossible and a meaningless demand.

In the meantime North Americans may as well realize that their own recent elections have certainly not been effective advertisements for the virtue or the necessity of the U.S. type of electoral process. To many intelligent Latin Americans, as well as to other nations of the hungry-nation bloc, they have seemed a race between two parties which differ little if at all on any real issues. To Cubans, they have also seemed a competition in belligerent ignorance about their country, rather than any reasonable public debate about actual problems Cubans—and the world—must now confront.

VI

The real political issue of Cuba and in Cuba seems to me to be this: Is it possible by revolutionary means of the sort being used in Cuba to build a genuinely free society? Is it possible to carry through in such drastic and rapid ways a revolution as fundamental as this one without producing either revolutionary terror or permanent dictatorship?

To my mind, these are not simple or unambiguous questions. How can they be, when the very meaning of "free society" is certainly quite open to debate? But I am unwilling—as are the Cuban revolutionaries—to identify "free society" only with the forms and mechanisms that have been historically developed in the United States or in various nations of Western Europe.

The historical record of the political outcomes of past revolutions is also ambiguous, but on the whole I think it leads one to pessimistic conclusions insofar as freedom is immediately concerned. The question is: Under what conditions can the Cuban revolution be different? No one can now truly answer this question. But let us consider briefly one comparison: Bolshevik Russia in about 1920 and Cuba today.

The internal situation of the Cuban Government is almost the precise opposite to that of the early Bolshevik Government. After a short visit to Russia, Bertrand Russell wrote in 1920: "The Government represents the interests of the urban and industrial population, and is, as it were, encamped amid a peasant nation, with whom its relations are rather diplomatic and military than governmental in the ordinary sense. . . . If Russia were governed democratically, according to the will of the majority, the inhabitants of Moscow and Petrograd would die of starvation."

In contrast, Cuba's Government today represents, above all, the interests of the people of the countryside, and moreover, it has managed to balance quite well these interests with those of the urban wage worker. There is no problem of food, which in the Russia of 1920 was indeed a terrible problem. The Cuban revolution, unlike the Russian, has, in my judgment, solved the major problems of agricultural production by its agrarian reform.

The early Soviet Government was under effective economic blockade: it could not procure things desperately needed from the outside, and its industry had virtually collapsed. Moreover, it was in full civil and external war. The energies of the industrial population were almost entirely devoted to this war, and the peasantry did not respond to the fact of the war or to the meaning of the blockade by the *Entente*. In all these respects, again, Cuba's situation is quite different. Cuba may feel menaced by the United States, but she is in fact not at war. Nor is she under any effective economic blockade: she is actively trading with many countries, including those of the Soviet bloc.

Of course, there are many other reasons why revolutions have led to reigns of terror and to long dictatorships. But in the case of the early Soviet Union, those I have mentioned were certainly among the most important. In this connection, I should also like to underline . . . the anti-Stalinist character of their general strategy of industrialization. . . . Moreover, in fact and in plan, those in charge of the industrialization of Cuba are very much aware of what they are doing and what they do not want to do. Continued economic progress, of just the sort that *is* being made in Cuba today, is a major condition leading us to a hopeful view of the political outcome of the revolution in Cuba.

VII

What impresses me most of all about the cultural possibilities in Cuba are the eagerness to learn and the openmindedness of many of the young men who make up the revolutionary Government of Cuba. In 20 years of teaching and writing, and of considerable travel, I have never before encountered such a sustained passion for learning, and such an intelligent awareness of the kinds of things that must be studied. And yet one of my major worries for Cuba is my worry for her cultural establishment. I do not mean only art and literature; I mean culture more broadly to include all those institutions of the mass media of communication and of higher and lower education by which the character and the mentality of men and women are formed.

The chief danger, I think, is quite simple: it is lack of qualified personnel. I mean this in two senses: first, in the ordinary sense of an absence of enough people with skill and knowledge and sensibility; but secondly, I am referring to this absence combined with the felt menace of counterrevolution and with the fact of a generally uneducated population. This combination *could* lead to the easy way out: the absolute control of all means of expression and the laying down of a Line to be followed.

Surely the more intelligent Cubans are correct . . . that at just this point above all others, the U.S.—as a Government or as a set of private individuals—could help mightily. The opportunity *is* there; in my view, it is not only an opportunity, it is a duty.

In their understandable euphoria about their educational accomplishments and plans, some Cubans, I think, tend to exaggerate the speed with which a truly educated personnel can be developed. Education of the sort needed in countries like Cuba, especially in the higher schools of learning, cannot now be provided by Cuban personnel. It is into *this* vacuum, and not into any military zone, that "extra-Hemispheric" forces are most likely to move and most likely, in my judgment, to be successful in their influences. The meaning of this fact for the United States is again obvious.

Yet I rather doubt that it is at all obvious to the people in charge of such matters in the United States. What intellectuals in Cuba are interested in, I doubt that the U.S. Department of State, as presently constituted, is *capable* of providing. For example, the interest of Cubans in all varieties of Marxism, in all varieties of left-wing thinking and politics, I find both understandable and admirable. For it is simply a fact that in practical and intellectual matters of the sort Cubans now confront, ideas of this sort are relevant; it is also a fact that the kinds of ideas officially acceptable in the United States, and approved by dominant sections of the U.S. intellectual community, are largely irrelevant, indeed often meaningless, for Cuban educational, administrative and cultural needs.

The North American public is generally ignorant of the varieties of left-wing thought and activity. At the same time it is true that some of the best and most scholarly studies of these subjects are now being carried on in our leading universities. Yet the result[s] of these studies do not get through to any larger public: they are confined to "specialists." That simple fact, I believe, is one reason why we cannot understand what the leaders and the peoples of the hungry-nation bloc are thinking, what they are trying to do, and what they are going to be thinking and doing in the future.

In the U.S. newspapers, all of it is simply lumped together as "communism," and communism is treated as an unchanging and homogeneous piece of evil.

The result for the citizen is plain ignorance about what most of the world is up to. It is the ignorance of the created provincial—intellectually and politically. Accordingly, it is no wonder that when events occur which cannot properly be understood, it leads to hysteria. The only insurance against such hysteria is knowledge—not the knowledge in one book or in a dozen books, but the knowledge that can only be provided by a genuinely free press whose management and whose journalists know what is important, know how to understand it and to explain it day by day and week by week. Such a press does not exist anywhere in the world.

That is one reason why the greatest thing for the cause of freedom any American foundation could do today would be to take up and to support, *in Cuban terms and under Cuban direction*, . . . a genuinely international university in Havana. And to follow it up by arranging publication in the United States, as well as elsewhere, of the continuing results of such a promising intellectual and political effort.

VIII

So again, we come back to the same theme: As we think about what is happening in Cuba and about the argument of the Cuban revolutionary, as we try to speculate well about the probabilities of Cuba's future, we are forced again and again to reflect upon the actual and the possible part in these matters by the United States of America. We cannot avoid this. It is a major element of Cuba's problems—and of Latin America's. And it is a major element of our problems as citizens of the United States.

No one can make up his mind about something like the Cuban revolution, or about U.S.-Cuban relations, without answering questions of a much larger scope. Two such questions seem to me immediately relevant:

1: Is it possible today to have a society that is economically just and sensible and at the same time politically fluent and free? This is an old question, an ultimate question, a continuing question—and no one knows the answer to it. Despite the burden of the Cuban past, and the consequences of U.S. policies—past and present—I believe that Cuba does now represent a real chance for the development of one form of such a society. (There are, of course, many possible forms.)

2: Is it politically possible, economically viable, and militarily realistic for a country such as Cuba to achieve a thoroughly neutralist and genuinely independent orientation in world affairs? Despite the systematic myopia of U.S. policies towards Cuba, and the astuteness of Soviet policy, I believe there is still a chance. To increase that chance, I believe, is the only realistic goal the United States can now take up in her Cuban policy.

When we deal with history, we are not dealing in certainties; we are dealing with chances. But in the case of Cuba today, we are dealing with chances in the outcome of which we are ourselves deeply involved.

It is not easy at this moment for North Americans to listen well to what the Cuban revolutionaries are saying about the world in which they live. But it is just this that we must do. We must see behind their revolutionary rhetoric to their purposes and to their accomplishments. We must understand that if they are exaggerating North American iniquities, their exaggerations are surely well balanced by North American spokesmen in their assertions about Cuba. Perhaps a little reflection would reveal that neither country is in the altogether sad condition imagined by spokesmen of the other. Above all, we must not allow our reactions to the *manner* of the Cuban accusations to hide from us the fact that many of their complaints about the United States, past and present, are solidly based upon historical and sociological fact. We must not believe that the genteel mannerisms of U.S. spokesmen are an answer to these complaints; on the contrary, we must realize that this pose is a way of escaping the argument. We must address ourselves to the very real basis of Cuba's case; we must answer—with fact, with reason, and with civilized policies—the argument of these revolutionaries of the hungry-nation bloc.

II. THE UNITED STATES RESPONSE TO CASTRO'S CUBA: THREE CRUCIAL EPISODES

Eisenhower and the Rupture of Diplomatic Relations

The first signs of Castro's opposition to the United States came only a few months after he had assumed power on January 1, 1959. Still a popular hero among the American people, the leader of the Cuban Revolution visited the United States in April. The details of his reception with American officials are still not known fully, but after Castro returned to Havana the diplomatic situation rapidly deteriorated. Americans voiced anger at the trials of former Batista henchmen, and the U.S. government firmly opposed Castro's nationalization laws, whereby foreign-owned companies were forced to submit to Cuban control. While the Eisenhower administration criticized Castro's trade arrangements with the Soviet Union, it secretly began planning to train and equip Cuban exiles for an invasion of the island. The following statements of the Eisenhower administration illustrate American concern and the drift towards an open break. Following the diplomatic rupture, Cuba accused the United States of plotting to invade the island and appealed for worldwide sympathy.

Dwight D. Eisenhower

STATEMENT BY THE PRESIDENT RESTATING

UNITED STATES POLICY TOWARD CUBA, JANUARY 26, 1960

SECRETARY [of State Christian] Herter and I have been giving careful consideration to the problem of relations between the Governments of the United States and Cuba. Ambassador [Philip] Bonsal, who is currently in Washington, shared in our discussions. We have been, for many months, deeply concerned and perplexed at the steady deterioration of those relations reflected especially by recent public statements by Prime Minister Castro of Cuba, as well as statements in official publicity organs of the Cuban Government. These statements contain unwarranted attacks on our Government and on our leading officials. These attacks involve serious charges none of which, however, has been the subject of formal representations by the Government of Cuba to our Government. We believe these charges to be totally unfounded.

We have prepared a re-statement of our policy toward Cuba, a country with whose people the people of the United States have enjoyed and expect to continue to enjoy a firm and mutually beneficial friendship.

The United States Government adheres strictly to the policy of nonintervention in the domestic affairs of other countries, including Cuba. This policy is

From *Public Papers of the Presidents of the United States: Dwight D. Eisenhower, 1960–1961* (Washington, 1961), pp. 134–136.

incorporated in our treaty commitments as a member of the Organization of American States.

Second, the United States Government has consistently endeavored to prevent illegal acts in territory under its jurisdiction directed against other governments. United States law enforcement agencies have been increasingly successful in the prevention of such acts. The United States record in this respect compares very favorably with that of Cuba from whose territory a number of invasions directed against other countries have departed during the past year, in several cases attended with serious loss of life and property damage in the territory of those other countries. The United States authorities will continue to enforce United States laws, including those which reflect commitments under Inter-American treaties, and hope that other governments will act similarly. Our Government has repeatedly indicated that it will welcome any information from the Cuban Government or from other governments regarding incidents occurring within their jurisdiction or notice, which would be of assistance to our law enforcement agencies in this respect.

Third, the United States Government views with increasing concern the tendency of spokesmen of the Cuban Government, including Prime Minister Castro, to create the illusion of aggressive acts and conspiratorial activities aimed at the Cuban Government and attributed to United States officials or agencies. The promotion of unfounded illusions of this kind can hardly facilitate the development, in the real interest of the two peoples, of relations of understanding and confidence between their governments. The United States Government regrets that its earnest efforts over the past year to establish a basis for such understanding and confidence have not been reciprocated.

Fourth, the United States Government, of course, recognizes the right of the Cuban Government and people in the exercise of their national sovereignty to undertake those social, economic and political reforms which, with due regard for their obligations under international law, they may think desirable. This position has frequently been stated and it reflects a real understanding of and sympathy with the ideals and aspirations of the Cuban people. Similarly, the United States Government and people will continue to assert and to defend, in the exercise of their own sovereignty, their legitimate interests.

Fifth, the United States Government believes that its citizens have made constructive contributions to the economies of other countries by means of their investments and their work in those countries and that such contributions, taking into account changing conditions, can continue on a mutually satisfactory basis. The United States Government will continue to bring to the attention of the Cuban Government any instances in which the rights of its citizens under Cuban law and under international law have been disregarded and in which redress under Cuban law is apparently unavailable or denied. In this connection it is the hope of the United States Government that differences of opinion between the two governments in matters recognized under international law as subject to diplomatic negotiations will be resolved through such negotiations. In the event that disagreements between the two governments concerning this matter should persist, it would be the intention of the United States Government to seek solutions through other appropriate international procedures.

The above points seem to me to furnish reasonable bases for a workable and satisfactory relationship between our two sovereign countries. I should like only to add that the United States Government has confidence in the ability of the Cuban people to recognize and defeat the intrigues of international communism which are aimed at destroying democratic institutions in Cuba and the traditional and mutually beneficial friendship between the Cuban and the American peoples.

REMARKS ON CUBA AND THE MONROE DOCTRINE AT THE PRESIDENT'S NEWS CONFERENCE, AUGUST 24, 1960

Q. Felix Belair, New York Times: Mr. President, in view of the indictment of the Castro regime by the American Republics foreign ministers, and particularly the United States white paper along this same line, do you consider that the Cuban problem is now beyond the realm of personal diplomacy, involving yourself; and as a second part, has the Monroe Doctrine been effectively supplanted by the Río and other non-intervention treaties?

The President: Well, let's take the second part. From my viewpoint, Mr. Belair, I think that the Monroe Doctrine has by no means been supplanted. It has been merely extended. When the Monroe Doctrine was written and enunciated, it had in mind such things as happened when the Austrians and the French—or an Austrian Emperor with some French troops—came into Mexico. Times have changed, and there are different kinds of penetration and subversion that can be very dangerous to the welfare of the OAS.

Now, the OAS is an organization that, for a long, long time we have been supporting, just as strongly as we can. We do want it to use its collective influence, its moral and political influence, in straightening out these things. But that does not, as I see it, inhibit any government, when it comes down to—when the chips are finally down, to looking after its own interests. They must be represented, of course—I mean they must be protected, of course.

STATEMENT BY THE PRESIDENT ON TERMINATING DIPLOMATIC RELATIONS WITH CUBA, JANUARY 3, 1961

BETWEEN one and two o'clock this morning, the Government of Cuba delivered to the United States Chargé d'Affaires ad interim of the United States Embassy in Habana a note stating that the Government of Cuba had decided to limit the personnel of our Embassy and Consulate in Habana to eleven persons. Forty-eight hours was granted for the departure of our entire staff with the exception of eleven. This unusual action on the part of the Castro Government can have no other purpose than to render impossible the conduct of normal diplomatic relations with that Government.

Accordingly, I have instructed the Secretary of State to deliver a note to the Chargé d'Affaires ad interim of Cuba in Washington which refers to the demand of his Government and states that the Government of the United States is hereby formally terminating diplomatic and consular relations with the Govern-

From *Public Papers of the Presidents of the United States: Dwight D. Eisenhower, 1960–1961* (Washington, 1961), p. 651.
From *Public Papers of the Presidents of the United States: Dwight D. Eisenhower, 1960–1961* (Washington, 1961), p. 891.

ment of Cuba. Copies of both notes are being made available to the press.

This calculated action on the part of the Castro Government is only the latest of a long series of harassments, baseless accusations, and vilification. There is a limit to what the United States in self-respect can endure. That limit has now been reached. Our friendship for the Cuban people is not affected. It is my hope and my conviction that in the not too distant future it will be possible for the historic friendship between us once again to find its reflection in normal relations of every sort. Meanwhile, our sympathy goes out to the people of Cuba now suffering under the yoke of a dictator.

Raúl Roa

CHARGES DELIVERED AGAINST THE UNITED STATES

BEFORE THE U.N. SECURITY COUNCIL, JANUARY 4, 1961

AT the very moment when Cuba is commemorating the second anniversary of its liberation, it is once again forced to turn to the Security Council to denounce in front of world public opinion the policy of harassment, reprisals, aggression, subversion, isolation, intervention and imminent military attack being carried out by the United States against the Government and people of Cuba, with the serious risk that this policy entails for international peace and security, which are already in a serious state because of increased tensions in Europe, Asia and Africa—and precisely as a result of the methods of interference, coercion and vacillation that are typical of the expiring Republican Administration in the conduct of its foreign relations.

Cuba is not alone. If its soil is attacked, the revolutionary Government and people of Cuba will have the assistance and support of those who have spontaneously committed themselves to defend Cuba's independence, self-determination, sovereignty and territorial integrity.

Cuba believes that the Security Council is the proper organ before which to bring our case, and that is why we have done so. We do not accept any jurisdiction other than the one chosen by us.

Furthermore, we believe that it is necessary to stress at this moment our opposition to any efforts to transfer the examination of our claim to the Organization of American States.

The blindest and most powerful enemy of the Cuban revolution has been and is the imperialist Government and reactionary group headed by President Eisenhower. They have fought against us since Fidel Castro began in Sierra Maestra to carry out the liberation, and we shall oppose this action until he leaves the White House and until Wall Street leaves us alone.

Now, at the end of his discredited and ruinous mandate, he has broken off diplomatic relations with Cuba and has approved the sinister plan of the Central Intelligence Agency to create conditions for military aggression against the Government and people of Cuba.

The pretexts that are used for the policy that is followed are the same as those that were used in the past since the time the revolution first took power—the transformation of Cuba into a spearhead of international communism; the setting up of a Communist government in Cuba; the granting of Cuban bases for the launching of Soviet rockets.

The purpose is obvious: to undermine and disfigure the character of the Cuban revolution in order to set the subjective and objective groundwork for direct military aggression; in other words, the glorious victory of Guatemala of 1954 is to be re-edited and repeated.

At this moment Cuba is immediately threatened with invasion by the United States. The initiative taken by the United States in breaking off relations with Cuba makes this imminence even more dramatic.

The Government and the people of Cuba are awaiting from one moment to the next the arrival of the invader. We know what they want us to do after the invasion. They want to restore by force the rotten regime which was overthrown by the revolution and to reimpose their degrading yoke of colonial domination.

Material from North America was airlifted to the counter-revolutionary groups operating in the mountains.

Officials of the United States Embassy in Havana were caught red-handed in their espionage activities. Camps of mercenaries are maintained in Florida and Central America and paid for with American dollars. The Central Intelligence Agency foots the bill for a systematic campaign of calumny from different broadcasting stations, and this part of the psychological warfare which has been unleashed in order to prepare conditions for a wide-scale assault.

The press spokesman of President Eisenhower stated on 29 October [1960] that the visit of the Marines to Guantánamo has been decided upon at the highest levels of the Administration with the full support of the Executive, and the fact was stressed that President Eisenhower had never previously been informed of the week-end rests that are given to Marines during their maneuvers.

Obviously, there was an interest in aggravating even further the tensions between the two countries by the new hostile episode, which also contributed to the preparation of conditions for direct military aggression.

Although the Central Intelligence Agency has very often changed its plans and postponed them, we have accurate information that we are now facing the final blow.

The mercenaries situated in Guantánamo are camouflaged in olive green uniforms with brown and white dots, like the ones used by the Marines in the Second World War. They are the best troops and they are the best armed.

The plan is to launch a number of small expeditions against different points of the island, synchronizing with attempts and actual sabotage in the cities. These expeditions will leave Florida and Swan Island.

While the landings are taking place the mercenaries stationed at Guantánamo Naval Base will leave for Sierra Maestra, from which they intend to attack a number of cities in Oriente Province, supported by aviation based in Guatemala and Swan Island.

The mercenaries also plan to bomb different points of Havana Province.

The war preparations which are being made in broad daylight, without any intention of hiding them, with a clear lack of respect for international laws, are articulated with an intense propaganda campaign, which is aimed at cracking the solid unity of the Cuban people.

The payment to these traitors who are working on these programs comes directly from the Administration in Washington. Not only do they carry out subversion but they also transmit orders in secret codes to the counter-revolutionaries, terrorists and saboteurs in Cuba, under the direction of the Central Intelligence Agency.

In order not to leave everything to the trustworthy reports of the Cuban Government, I shall turn to the *U.S. News & World Report*, which prides itself on discovering international criminals in their illegitimate activities. According to this magazine, one of the groups implicated in this eagerness to obtain Federal dollars has a very luxurious home in Miami devoted to the preparation of those radio programs, which are taped there and then broadcast from a thirty-five foot vessel which is based in the Southern city.

In March of this year [1960], President Eisenhower traveled all over South America. The question of Cuba was consistently part of his agenda. He applied personal diplomacy, and although I do not know what harvest he gathered in official circles, the public one is well known; he was greeted with a symphony of whistlings that shook his ears every time he went through the main urban areas of our America. Only Vice President Nixon was able to compete with him in this climate of hostility that accompanied him in his trip and which froze his famous smile.

It has been stated falsely that Cuba is the satellite of international communism, but the truth is different. Cuba has ceased forever to be a satellite of American imperialism, and it is for this reason that we are accused of being Communists.

Unable, in its blindness, to understand the profound and vast changes that are taking place in present-day society, American imperialism can consider only one alternative: either its satellite or another's. And, since it does not admit any relation with other peoples except submission, it can only accept such submission unconditionally.

Since we have rejected this opprobrious servitude, American imperialism is trying to break down our Government by means of harassment, pressure, threats, reprisals and aggression. But it could not do this. It tried to break Cuba's back by hunger. Now it is trying to stop Cuba's revolutionary impulse by force.

But Cuba owes its survival in this crucial moment of its history to the unshakable determination of the revolutionary Government and to the prodigious courage of its people, and, secondly, to the friendly countries that gave it help without insisting on subordination of political commitments.

Cuba was able to overcome the economic catastrophe to which it was condemned by the Government of the United States, thanks to the economic, commercial and technical cooperation of the Soviet Union, the People's Republics of China, Czechoslovakia, Poland, Yugoslavia, the United Arab Republic, Japan and Canada, and, as an encouragement, we now count upon the solidarity and support of all the peoples of Latin America, Africa, and Asia. I say again that Cuba does not stand alone. And thus I repeat that Cuba will fight to win or die, and we shall fight—and not alone.

We do not want to provoke the suicide of humanity but, if an atomic conflagration were to be unleashed because of the military intervention in Cuba, the responsibility would fall squarely on the imperialist and reactionary Government of General Eisenhower. It would in truth be monstrous to unleash on the world, in order to serve capitalist aims and colonial exploitation, the devastating effects of a nuclear war.

The fragile ties which still link the revolutionary government of Cuba with the imperialist and reactionary government of President Eisenhower were terminated when he broke off diplomatic relations with Cuba last night. We are not unaware of the fact that that breaking off will precipitate aggression. But, fortunately, the snake pit that was the American Embassy in Cuba was also wiped out.

In the present circumstances, it seems obvious that the revolutionary Government of Cuba rejects in advance any draft resolution which prescribes any type of understanding with the imperialist and reactionary Government of President Eisenhower. There is no possible common ground between the two. The reactionary and imperialist Government of President Eisenhower has already decreed military intervention against Cuba and Cuba is ready to expel it.

There is only one way of characterizing this ignoble international conduct and that is to declare it the conduct of an aggressor. It is that which, on behalf of the Government and people of Cuba, I ask of the Security Council.

James Wadsworth

REPLY TO RAÚL ROA

BEGINNING in the spring and summer of 1959 a series of invasion attempts upset the peace of the Caribbean area. Panama, Nicaragua, the Dominican Republic, and Haiti were the victims. In every case it has been established beyond reasonable doubt that the expeditions had the support of Cuban officials. In the case of the invasion of Panama in June of 1959, the investigating committee appointed by the Council of the Organization of American States studied the facts and concluded that—and I quote from their report—"the Republic of Panama was the victim of an invasion organized abroad that sailed from a Cuban port and was composed entirely of foreigners." In fact, the chairman of the committee was able to confirm that 82 out of the 84 invaders who were taken prisoner were Cubans. The invasions of Haiti were apparently attempted with the complicity of the Cuban Ambassador there and his five military attachés.

Finally, Mr. President, by plunging their country into this subversive and military activity which is far beyond the resources of Cuba acting alone, the leaders of Cuba have put that unhappy country more and more into the hands of international communism.

Last February, when the First Deputy Premier of the Soviet Union, Mr. [Anastas I.] Mikoyan, visited Cuba, a communiqué was issued in Habana about Mr. Mikoyan's conversations with the Cuban leaders. It contained this statement: "Expression was given to the constant striving of both governments to implement active and joint activity in the United Nations." We have already seen evidences of that joint activity—not only today but as when, last September, the General Assembly voted on a Soviet proposal for a plenary debate on its discredited charge of United States aerial aggression. There were only 10 votes for that proposal: the 9 votes of the Soviet bloc, which virtually always votes together, and—Cuba.

And now, Mr. President, I submit that we see another example of that "joint activity" right here in the Council. It has been remarked to me, and I think truly, that the Soviet Union must find it very convenient that the Security Council should be hearing this spurious Cuban charge of an imaginary United States aggression at a point when world opinion might otherwise be noticing certain events in Laos or in the Congo.

Such is the record of Cuba's self-isolation in the past 2 years. What began 2 years ago as a bright hope for the Cuban people, applauded widely by the American people and by the Eisenhower administration, as well as throughout the world, quickly turned into a reign of terror at home and thence into a danger to the peace and freedom of the entire hemisphere.

Now, Mr. President, severely provoked though we are, as last night's action will attest, the United States' aims regarding Cuba have not changed. In the face of this situation we shall cooperate with our allies in the Western Hemisphere to help maintain its security against aggression from whatever source.

And we will never cease to look for a way back to peace and friendship between Cuba and the United States.

From James Wadsworth, "Reply to Raúl Roa," Department of State Bulletin, XLIV (January 23, 1961), p. 107.

The Bay of Pigs, April, 1961

On January 20, 1961, the new chief executive, John F. Kennedy, inherited invasion plans prepared during the last months of the Eisenhower administration. During the first months of the new administration, Kennedy debated the merits of the Central Intelligence Agency proposal for invading Cuba. In the end, the young President reluctantly accepted the argument that only Cuban exiles were going to fight, and that the invasion team, in training in Central America, was ready to strike. From the beginning everything went wrong. Castro's air force survived a pre-invasion attack, and, once the exiles hit the beaches at the Bay of Pigs, they were quickly stranded. Their defeat marked a low point in Kennedy's prestige in Latin America, and his program in the Alliance for Progress was now suspect. In December a jubilant Fidel Castro announced his commitment to Marxism-Leninism. Cuba, as the following selections show, was now a Cold War issue.

THE STATE DEPARTMENT'S DEFENSE OF U.S. POLICY

THE present situation in Cuba confronts the Western Hemisphere and the inter-American system with a grave and urgent challenge.

This challenge does not result from the fact that the Castro government in Cuba was established by revolution. The hemisphere rejoiced at the overthrow of the Batista tyranny, looked with sympathy on the new regime, and welcomed its promises of political freedom and social justice for the Cuban people. The challenge results from the fact that the leaders of the revolutionary regime betrayed their own revolution, delivered that revolution into the hands of powers alien to the hemisphere, and transformed it into an instrument employed with calculated effect to suppress the rekindled hopes of the Cuban people for democracy and to intervene in the internal affairs of other American Republics.

What began as a movement to enlarge Cuban democracy and freedom has been perverted, in short, into a mechanism for the destruction of free institutions in Cuba, for the seizure by international communism of a base and bridgehead in the Americas, and for the disruption of the inter-American system.

It is the considered judgment of the Government of the United States of America that the Castro regime in Cuba offers a clear and present danger to the authentic and autonomous revolution of the Americas—to the whole hope of spreading political liberty, economic development, and social progress through all the republics of the hemisphere.

*   *   *

In place of the democratic spontaneity of the Cuban Revolution, Dr. Castro placed his confidence in the ruthless discipline of the Cuban Communist Party. Today that party is the *only* political party permitted to operate in Cuba. Today its members and those responsive to its influence dominate the government of Cuba, the commissions

From *Cuba*, Department of State Publication 7171, Inter-American Series 66 (April, 1961), pp. 1–2, 11, 25–26, 33–36.

of economic planning, the labor front, the press, the educational system, and all the agencies of national power.

*   *   *

The transformation of Cuba into a Soviet satellite is, from the viewpoint of the Cuban leaders, not an end but a beginning. Dr. Castro's fondest dream is a continent-wide upheaval which would reconstruct all Latin America on the model of Cuba. "We promise," he said on July 26, 1960, "to continue making the nation the example that can convert the Cordillera of the Andes into the Sierra Maestra of the hemisphere." "If they want to accuse us of wanting a revolution in all America," he added later, "let them accuse us."

Under Castro, Cuba has already become a base and staging area for revolutionary activity throughout the continent. In prosecuting the war against the hemisphere, Cuban embassies in Latin American countries work in close collaboration with Iron Curtain diplomatic missions and with the Soviet intelligence services. In addition, Cuban expressions of fealty to the Communist world have provided the Soviet Government a long-sought pretext for threats of direct interventions of its own in the Western Hemisphere. "We shall do everything to support Cuba in her struggle," Prime Minister Khrushchev said on July 9, 1960, ". . . Speaking figuratively, in case of necessity, Soviet artillerymen can support with rocket fire the Cuban people if aggressive forces in the Pentagon dare to start intervention against Cuba."

*   *   *

It is not clear whether Dr. Castro intended from the start to betray his pledges of a free and democratic Cuba, to deliver his country to the Sino-Soviet bloc, and to mount an attack on the inter-American system; or whether he made his original pledges in all sincerity but, on assuming his new responsibilities, found himself increasingly dependent on ruthless men around him with clear

ideas and the disciplined organization to carry those ideas into action. What is important is not the motive but the result.

The first result has been the institution of a repressive dictatorship in Cuba.

The existence of a regime dedicated to so calculated an attack on human decencies would by itself be a sufficient occasion for intense concern within the hemisphere. In recent years the American family of nations has moved steadily toward the conclusion that the safety and welfare of all the American Republics will be best protected by the establishment and guarantee within each republic of what the OAS Charter calls "the essential rights of man."

But Dr. Castro has done more than establish a dictatorship in Cuba; he has committed that dictatorship to a totalitarian movement outside the hemisphere.

Just as the American Republics over 20 years ago, in conferences beginning at Lima in 1938 and culminating at Río de Janeiro in 1942, proclaimed that they could not tolerate the invasion of the hemisphere and the seizure of the American States by Nazi movements, serving the interests of the German Reich, so today they reject such invasion and seizure by Communist movements serving the interests of the Sino-Soviet bloc.

The people of Cuba remain our brothers. We acknowledge past omissions and errors in our relationship to them. The United States, along with the other nations of the hemisphere, expresses a profound determination to assure future democratic governments in Cuba full and positive support in their efforts to help the Cuban people achieve freedom, democracy, and social justice.

We call once again on the Castro regime to sever its links with the international Communist movement, to return to the original purposes which brought so many gallant men together in the Sierra Maestra, and to restore the integrity of the Cuban Revolution.

If this call is unheeded, we are confident that the Cuban people, with their passion for liberty, will continue to strive for a free Cuba; that they will return to the splendid vision of inter-American unity and progress; and that in the spirit of José Martí they will join hands with the other republics in the hemisphere in the struggle to win freedom.

Because the Castro regime has become the spearhead of attack on the inter-American system, that regime represents a fateful challenge to the inter-American system. For freedom is the common destiny of our hemisphere—freedom *from* domestic tyranny and foreign intervention, *from* hunger and poverty and illiteracy, freedom *for* each person and nation in the Americas to realize the high potentialities of life in the twentieth century.

THE SOVIET FOREIGN OFFICE'S STATEMENT

ON THE BAY OF PIGS INVASION

THE Government of the Republic of Cuba has announced that in the morning of 15 April [1961] airplanes of the U.S. B–26 bomber type subjected separate districts of the capital of Cuba—Havana—and a number of other inhabited localities to barbarous bombing. There were many killed and injured among the inhabitants of the capital.

Following the bombing, early in the morning of 17 April armed forces of the interventionists landed at various places on the Cuban coast. The landing took place under the cover of U.S. aircraft and warships.

Cuban Government troops and the People's Militia are engaged in fighting the invading gangs.

In connection with the invasion of Cuba the Government of the Soviet Union states:

The attack on Cuba is an open challenge to all freedom-loving peoples, a dangerous provocation against peace in the area of the Caribbean Sea, against universal peace. There can be no justification of this criminal invasion. The organizers of the aggression against Cuba are encroaching on the inalienable right of the Cuban people to live freely and independently. They are trampling underfoot the elementary norms of international relations, the principles of peaceful coexistence of states.

The Cuban nation has not threatened and is not threatening anyone. Having overthrown the tyranny of the bloody despot Batista, lackey of the big U.S. monopolies, the Cuban nation has embarked upon the pursuit of an independent policy, of raising its economy, and improving its life. It demands to be left in peace, to be left to build its life in conformity with its national ideals.

Can small Cuba with its population of 6 million threaten anyone—and such a big state as the United States at that? Of course not. Yet since the first days of the victory of the national revolution in Cuba the United States became the center where the counterrevolutionary elements thrown out from Cuba gathered, where they were formed into gangs and armed for struggle against the popular government of Fidel Castro. Recent events show that the present U.S. Government, which declared itself heir to Roosevelt's policy, is in essence pursuing the reactionary imperialist policy of Dulles and Eisenhower so condemned by the nations.

The U.S. Government declared through President Kennedy that the basic controversial question on Cuba is not a matter of a quarrel between the United States and Cuba but concerns the Cubans alone. The President said that he advocated a free and independent Cuba. In fact, however, everything was done on the territory of the United States

From the Department of State Bulletin, XLIV (May 8, 1961), pp. 662–663.

and the countries dependent on it to prepare an aggressive attack on Cuba. But for the open aggressive policy of the United States towards Cuba would the counterrevolutionary gangs of the hirelings of U.S. capital have been able to create the so-called Cuban Government on U.S. territory? What territory served as a starting point for the piratical attack on Cuba?

It was the territory of the United States and that of the neighboring countries which are under its control. Whose are the arms with which the counterrevolutionary gangs are equipped? They are U.S. arms. With whose funds have they been supported and are they being maintained? With funds appropriated by the United States.

It is clear from this that it is precisely the United States which is the inspirer and organizer of the present bandit-like attack on Cuba. Why did the United States organize this criminal attack on the Cuban Republic? Because, after the overthrow of the tyranny of Batista, the Cuban people were finished with the plunder and exploitation of their homeland by foreign monopolies. These monopolies do not wish to concede anything to the people of Cuba, the peoples of Latin America. They fear that Cuba, building its independent life, will become an example for other countries of Latin America. With the hands of base mercenaries they want to take from the Cuban people their right to determine their own fate, as they did with Guatemala.

But every nation has the right to live as it wishes, and no one, no state has the right to impose its own way of life on other nations. The Cuban nation has passed through a long, harsh, and difficult school of struggle for its freedom and independence against foreign oppressors and their accomplices, and it will not be brought to its knees, will not permit the yoke of foreign enslavers to be placed upon its shoulders. All progressive mankind, all upright people are on the side of Cuba.

The Government of the Soviet Union states that the Soviet Union, as other peace-loving countries, will not abandon the Cuban people in their trouble nor will it refuse it all necessary aid and support in the just struggle for the freedom and independence of Cuba.

The Soviet Government, at this crucial moment, for the sake of preserving universal peace, appeals to the Government of the United States to take measures to stop the aggression against Cuba and intervention in Cuba's internal affairs. Protection of and aid to the counterrevolutionary bands must be stopped immediately.

The Soviet Government hopes that it will be understood in the United States that aggression goes against the interests of the American people and is capable of jeopardizing the peaceful life of the population of the United States itself.

The Soviet Government demands urgent study by the U.N. General Assembly of the question of aggressive actions of the United States, which has prepared and unleashed armed intervention against Cuba.

The Government of the U.S.S.R. appeals to the governments of all member states of the United Nations to take all necessary measures for the immediate cessation of aggressive actions against Cuba, the continuation of which may give rise to the most serious consequences for universal peace.

In this hour, when the sovereignty and independence of Cuba, a sovereign member of the United Nations, are in danger, the duty of all countries members of the United Nations is to render it all necessary aid and support.

The Soviet Government reserves the right, if armed intervention in the affairs of the Cuban people is not stopped, to take all measures with other countries to render the necessary assistance to the Republic of Cuba.

John F. Kennedy

ADDRESS BEFORE THE AMERICAN SOCIETY OF

NEWSPAPER EDITORS, APRIL 20, 1961

THE President of a great democracy such as ours, and the editors of great newspapers such as yours, owe a common obligation to the people: an obligation to present the facts, to present them with candor, and to present them in perspective. It is with that obligation in mind that I have decided in the last 24 hours to discuss briefly at this time the recent events in Cuba.

On that unhappy island, as in so many other arenas of the contest for freedom, the news has grown worse instead of better. I have emphasized before that this was a struggle of Cuban patriots against a Cuban dictator. While we could not be expected to hide our sympathies, we made it repeatedly clear that the armed forces of this country would not intervene in any way.

Any unilateral American intervention, in the absence of an external attack upon ourselves or an ally, would have been contrary to our traditions and to our international obligations. But let the record show that our restraint is not inexhaustible. Should it ever appear that the inter-American doctrine of non-interference merely conceals or excuses a policy of nonaction—if the nations of this Hemisphere should fail to meet their commitments against outside Communist penetration—then I want it clearly understood that this Government will not hesitate in meeting its primary obligations which are to the security of our Nation!

Should that time ever come, we do not intend to be lectured on "intervention" by those whose character was stamped for all time on the bloody streets of Budapest! Nor would we expect or accept the same outcome which this small band of gallant Cuban refugees must have known that they were chancing, determined as they were against heavy odds to pursue their courageous attempts to regain their Island's freedom.

But Cuba is not an island unto itself; and our concern is not ended by mere expressions of nonintervention or regret. This is not the first time in either ancient or recent history that a small band of freedom fighters has engaged the armor of totalitarianism.

It is not the first time that Communist tanks have rolled over gallant men and women fighting to redeem the independence of their homeland. Nor is it by any means the final episode in the eternal struggle of liberty against tyranny, anywhere on the face of the globe, including Cuba itself.

Mr. Castro has said that these were mercenaries. According to press reports, the final message to be relayed from the refugee forces on the beach came from the rebel commander when asked if he wished to be evacuated. His answer was: "I will never leave this country." That is not the reply of a mercenary. He has gone now to join in the mountains countless other guerrilla fighters, who are equally determined that the dedication of those who gave their lives shall not be forgotten, and that Cuba must not be abandoned to the Communists. And we do not intend to abandon it either!

The Cuban people have not yet spoken their final piece. And I have no doubt that they and their Revolutionary Council, led by Dr. [José Miró] Cardona—and

From *Public Papers of the Presidents of the United States: John F. Kennedy, 1961* (Washington, 1962), pp. 304–306.

members of the families of the Revolutionary Council, I am informed by the Doctor yesterday, are involved themselves in the Islands—will continue to speak up for a free and independent Cuba.

Meanwhile we will not accept Mr. Castro's attempts to blame this nation for the hatred with which his onetime supporters now regard his repression. But there are from this sobering episode useful lessons for us all to learn. Some may be still obscure, and await further information. Some are clear today.

First, it is clear that the forces of communism are not to be underestimated, in Cuba or anywhere else in the world. The advantages of a police state—its use of mass terror and arrests to prevent the spread of free dissent—cannot be overlooked by those who expect the fall of every fanatic tyrant. If the self-discipline of the free cannot match the iron discipline of the mailed fist—in economic, political, scientific and all the other kinds of struggles as well as the military —then the peril to freedom will continue to rise.

Secondly, it is clear that this Nation, in concert with all the free nations of this hemisphere, must take an ever closer and more realistic look at the menace of external Communist intervention and domination in Cuba. The American people are not complacent about Iron Curtain tanks and planes less than 90 miles from their shore. But a nation of Cuba's size is less a threat to our survival than it is a base for subverting the survival of other free nations throughout the hemisphere. It is not primarily our interest or our security but theirs which is now, today, in the greater peril. It is for their sake as well as our own that we must show our will.

The evidence is clear—and the hour is late. We and our Latin friends will have to face the fact that we cannot postpone any longer the real issue of survival of freedom in this hemisphere itself. On that issue, unlike perhaps some others, there can be no middle ground. Together we must build a hemisphere where freedom can flourish; and where any free nation under outside attack of any kind can be assured that all of our resources stand ready to respond to any request for assistance.

Third, and finally, it is clearer than ever that we face a relentless struggle in every corner of the globe that goes far beyond the clash of armies or even nuclear armaments. The armies are there, and in large number. The nuclear armaments are there. But they serve primarily as the shield behind which subversion, infiltration, and a host of other tactics steadily advance, picking off vulnerable areas one by one in situations which do not permit our own armed intervention.

Power is the hallmark of this offensive —power and discipline and deceit. The legitimate discontent of yearning people is exploited. The legitimate trappings of self-determination are employed. But once in power, all talk of discontent is repressed, all self-determination disappears, and the promise of a revolution of hope is betrayed, as in Cuba, into a reign of terror. Those who on instruction staged automatic "riots" in the streets of free nations over the efforts of a small group of young Cubans to regain their freedom should recall the long roll call of refugees who cannot now go back—to Hungary, to North Korea, to North Viet-Nam, to East Germany, or to Poland, or to any of the other lands from which a steady stream of refugees pours forth, in eloquent testimony to the cruel oppression now holding sway in their homeland.

We dare not fail to see the insidious nature of this new and deeper struggle. We dare not fail to grasp the new concepts, the new tools, the new sense of urgency we will need to combat it— whether in Cuba or South Viet-Nam. And we dare not fail to realize that this struggle is taking place every day, without fanfare, in thousands of villages and markets—day and night—and in classrooms all over the globe.

The message of Cuba, of Laos, of the rising din of Communist voices in Asia and Latin America—these messages are all the same. The complacent, the self-indulgent, the soft societies are about to be swept away with the debris of history.

Only the strong, only the industrious, only the determined, only the courageous, only the visionary who determine the real nature of our struggle can possibly survive.

No greater task faces this country or this administration. No other challenge is more deserving of our every effort and energy. Too long we have fixed our eyes on traditional military needs, on armies prepared to cross borders, on missiles poised for flight. Now it should be clear that this is no longer enough—that our security may be lost piece by piece, country by country, without the firing of a single missile or the crossing of a single border.

We intend to profit from this lesson. We intend to reexamine and reorient our forces of all kinds—our tactics and our institutions here in this community. We intend to intensify our efforts for a struggle in many ways more difficult than war, where disappointment will often accompany us.

For I am convinced that we in this country and in the free world possess the necessary resource, and the skill, and the added strength that comes from a belief in the freedom of man. And I am equally convinced that history will record the fact that this bitter struggle reached its climax in the late 1950's and the early 1960's. Let me then make clear as the President of the United States that I am determined upon our system's survival and success, regardless of the cost and regardless of the peril!

The Missile Crisis, October, 1962

No one can be sure what motivated Castro to sign the pact with the Soviet Union providing for the installation of missiles in Cuba. Perhaps it was concluded at Castro's behest as a means to protect Cuba from another Bay of Pigs. Perhaps Nikita Khrushchev thought he saw a chance to alter the nuclear balance of power. Throughout the summer of 1962 Cuban exiles voiced accusations that unusual military activity was underway in remote areas of the island. Kennedy, already sensitive to the charges of meddling in Latin-American politics, was determined to wait for proof. Conclusive evidence came only in mid-October, 1962. The next few weeks witnessed the most dangerous hours of the Cold War. The President appointed a special task force to develop strategy and announced the quarantine decision in the famous speech on October 22. The selections below trace the debate in the United Nations and Khrushchev's capitulation.

John F. Kennedy

CUBAN MISSILE CRISIS SPEECH, OCTOBER 22, 1962

GOOD evening, my fellow citizens: This Government, as promised, has maintained the closest surveillance of the Soviet military buildup on the island of Cuba. Within the past week, unmistakable evidence has established the fact that a series of offensive missile sites is now in preparation on that imprisoned

From *Public Papers of the Presidents of the United States: John F. Kennedy, 1962* (Washington, 1963), pp. 806–809.

island. The purpose of these bases can be none other than to provide a nuclear strike capability against the Western Hemisphere.

Upon receiving the first preliminary hard information of this nature last Tuesday morning at 9 A.M., I directed that our surveillance be stepped up. And having now confirmed and completed our evaluation of the evidence and our decision on a course of action, this Government feels obliged to report this new crisis to you in fullest detail.

The characteristics of these new missile sites indicate two distinct types of installations. Several of them include medium range ballistic missiles, capable of carrying a nuclear warhead for a distance of more than 1,000 nautical miles. Each of these missiles, in short, is capable of striking Washington, D.C., the Panama Canal, Cape Canaveral, Mexico City, or any other city in the southeastern part of the United States, in Central America, or in the Caribbean area.

Additional sites not yet completed appear to be designed for intermediate range ballistic missiles—capable of traveling more than twice as far—and thus capable of striking most of the major cities in the Western Hemisphere, ranging as far north as Hudson Bay, Canada, and as far south as Lima, Peru. In addition, jet bombers, capable of carrying nuclear weapons, are now being uncrated and assembled in Cuba, while the necessary air bases are being prepared.

This urgent transformation of Cuba into an important strategic base—by the presence of these large, long-range, and clearly offensive weapons of sudden mass destruction—constitutes an explicit threat to the peace and security of all the Americas, in flagrant and deliberate defiance of the Río Pact of 1947, the traditions of this Nation and hemisphere, the joint resolution of the 87th Congress, the Charter of the United Nations, and my own public warnings to the Soviets on September 4 and 13. This action also contradicts the repeated assurances of Soviet spokesmen, both publicly and privately delivered, that the arms buildup in Cuba would retain its original defensive character, and that

the Soviet Union had no need or desire to station strategic missiles on the territory of any other nation.

The size of this undertaking makes clear that it has been planned for some months. Yet only last month, after I had made clear the distinction between any introduction of ground-to-ground missiles and the existence of defensive antiaircraft missiles, the Soviet Government publicly stated on September 11 that, and I quote, "the armaments and military equipment sent to Cuba are designed exclusively for defensive purposes," that, and I quote the Soviet Government, "there is no need for the Soviet Government to shift its weapons . . . for a retaliatory blow to any other country, for instance Cuba," and that, and I quote their government, "the Soviet Union has so powerful rockets to carry these nuclear warheads that there is no need to search for sites for them beyond the boundaries of the Soviet Union." That statement was false.

Only last Thursday, as evidence of this rapid offensive buildup was already in my hand, Soviet Foreign Minister [Andrei] Gromyko told me in my office that he was instructed to make it clear once again, as he said his government had already done, that Soviet assistance to Cuba, and I quote, "pursued solely the purpose of contributing to the defense capabilities of Cuba," that, and I quote him, "training by Soviet specialists of Cuban nationals in handling defensive armaments was by no means offensive, and if it were otherwise," Mr. Gromyko went on, "the Soviet Government would never become involved in rendering such assistance." That statement also was false.

Neither the United States of America nor the world community of nations can tolerate deliberate deception and offensive threats on the part of any nation, large or small. We no longer live in a world where only the actual firing of weapons represents a sufficient challenge to a nation's security to constitute maximum peril. Nuclear weapons are so destructive and ballistic missiles are so swift, that any substantially increased possibility of their use or any sudden change in their deployment may well be regarded as a definite threat to peace.

For many years, both the Soviet Union and the United States, recognizing this fact, have deployed strategic nuclear weapons with great care, never upsetting the precarious status quo which insured that these weapons would not be used in the absence of some vital challenge. Our own strategic missiles have never been transferred to the territory of any other nation under a cloak of secrecy and deception; and our history —unlike that of the Soviets since the end of World War II—demonstrates that we have no desire to dominate or conquer any other nation or impose our system upon its people. Nevertheless, American citizens have become adjusted to living daily on the bull's-eye of Soviet missiles located inside the U.S.S.R. or in submarines.

In that sense, missiles in Cuba add to an already clear and present danger— although it should be noted the nations of Latin America have never previously been subjected to a potential nuclear threat.

But this secret, swift, and extraordinary buildup of Communist missiles— in an area well known to have a special and historical relationship to the United States and the nations of the Western Hemisphere, in violation of Soviet assurances, and in defiance of American and hemispheric policy—this sudden, clandestine decision to station strategic weapons for the first time outside of Soviet soil—is a deliberately provocative and unjustified change in the status quo which cannot be accepted by this country, if our courage and our commitments are ever to be trusted again by either friend or foe.

The 1930's taught us a clear lesson: aggressive conduct, if allowed to go unchecked and unchallenged, ultimately leads to war. This nation is opposed to war. We are also true to our word. Our unswerving objective, therefore, must be to prevent the use of these missiles against this or any other country, and to secure their withdrawal or elimination from the Western Hemisphere.

Our policy has been one of patience and restraint, as befits a peaceful and powerful nation, which leads a worldwide alliance. We have been determined not to be diverted from our central concerns by mere irritants and fanatics. But now further action is required—and it is under way; and these actions may only be the beginning. We will not prematurely or unnecessarily risk the costs of worldwide nuclear war in which even the fruits of victory would be ashes in our mouth—but neither will we shrink from that risk at any time it must be faced.

Acting, therefore, in the defense of our own security and of the entire Western Hemisphere, and under the authority entrusted to me by the Constitution as endorsed by the resolution of the Congress, I have directed that the following *initial* steps be taken immediately:

First: To halt this offensive buildup, a strict quarantine on all offensive military equipment under shipment to Cuba is being initiated. All ships of any kind bound for Cuba from whatever nation or port will, if found to contain cargoes of offensive weapons, be turned back. This quarantine will be extended, if needed, to other types of cargo and carriers. We are not at this time, however, denying the necessities of life as the Soviets attempted to do in their Berlin blockade of 1948.

Second: I have directed the continued and increased close surveillance of Cuba and its military buildup. The foreign ministers of the OAS, in their communiqué of October 6, rejected secrecy on such matters in this hemisphere. Should these offensive military preparations continue, thus increasing the threat to the hemisphere, further action will be justified. I have directed the Armed Forces to prepare for any eventualities; and I trust that in the interest of both the Cuban people and the Soviet technicians at the sites, the hazards to all concerned of continuing this threat will be recognized.

Third: It shall be the policy of this Nation to regard any nuclear missile launched from Cuba against any nation in the Western Hemisphere as an attack by the Soviet Union on the United States, requiring a full retaliatory response upon the Soviet Union.

Fourth: As a necessary military precaution, I have reinforced our base at Guantánamo, evacuated today the dependents of our personnel there, and ordered additional military units to be on a standby alert basis.

Fifth: We are calling tonight for an immediate meeting of the Organ of Consultation under the Organization of American States, to consider this threat to hemispheric security and to invoke articles 6 and 8 of the Río Treaty in support of all necessary action. The United Nations Charter allows for regional security arrangements—and the nations of this hemisphere decided long ago against the military presence of outside powers. Our other allies around the world have also been alerted.

Sixth: Under the Charter of the United Nations, we are asking tonight that an emergency meeting of the Security Council be convoked without delay to take action against this latest Soviet threat to world peace. Our resolution will call for the prompt dismantling and withdrawal of all offensive weapons in Cuba, under the supervision of U.N. observers, before the quarantine can be lifted.

Seventh and finally: I call upon Chairman Khrushchev to halt and eliminate this clandestine, reckless, and provocative threat to world peace and to stable relations between our two nations. I call upon him further to abandon this course of world domination, and to join in an historic effort to end the perilous arms race and to transform the history of man. He has an opportunity now to move the world back from the abyss of destruction —by returning to his government's own words that it had no need to station missiles outside its own territory, and withdrawing these weapons from Cuba—by refraining from any action which will widen or deepen the present crisis—and then by participating in a search for peaceful and permanent solutions.

This Nation is prepared to present its case against the Soviet threat to peace, and our own proposals for a peaceful world, at any time and in any forum—in the OAS, in the United Nations, or in any other meeting that could be useful— without limiting our freedom of action. We have in the past made strenuous efforts to limit the spread of nuclear weapons. We have proposed the elimination of all arms and military bases in a fair and effective disarmament treaty. We are prepared to discuss new proposals for the removal of tensions on both sides— including the possibilities of a genuinely independent Cuba, free to determine its own destiny. We have no wish to war with the Soviet Union—for we are a peaceful people who desire to live in peace with all other peoples.

But it is difficult to settle or even discuss these problems in an atmosphere of intimidation. That is why this latest Soviet threat—or any other threat which is made either independently or in response to our actions this week—must and will be met with determination. Any hostile move anywhere in the world against the safety and freedom of peoples to whom we are committed—including in particular the brave people of West Berlin—will be met by whatever action is needed.

Finally, I want to say a few words to the captive people of Cuba, to whom this speech is being directly carried by special radio facilities. I speak to you as a friend, as one who knows of your deep attachment to your fatherland, as one who shares your aspirations for liberty and justice for all. And I have watched and the American people have watched with deep sorrow how your nationalist revolution was betrayed—and how your fatherland fell under foreign domination. Now your leaders are no longer Cuban leaders inspired by Cuban ideals. They are puppets and agents of an international conspiracy which has turned Cuba against your friends and neighbors in the Americas—and turned it into the first Latin American country to become a target for nuclear war—the first Latin American country to have these weapons on its soil.

These new weapons are not in your

interest. They contribute nothing to your peace and well-being. They can only undermine it. But this country has no wish to cause you to suffer or to impose any system upon you. We know that your lives and land are being used as pawns by those who deny your freedom.

Many times in the past, the Cuban people have risen to throw out tyrants who destroyed their liberty. And I have no doubt that most Cubans today look forward to the time when they will be truly free—free from foreign domination, free to choose their own leaders, free to select their own system, free to own their own land, free to speak and write and worship without fear or degradation. And then shall Cuba be welcomed back to the society of free nations and to the associations of this hemisphere.

My fellow citizens: let no one doubt that this is a difficult and dangerous effort on which we have set out. No one can foresee precisely what course it will take or what costs or casualties will be incurred. Many months of sacrifice and self-discipline lie ahead—months in which both our patience and our will will be tested—months in which many threats and denunciations will keep us aware of our dangers. But the greatest danger of all would be to do nothing.

The path we have chosen for the present is full of hazards, as all paths are—but it is the one most consistent with our character and courage as a nation and our commitments around the world. The cost of freedom is always high—but Americans have always paid it. And one path we shall never choose, and that is the path of surrender or submission.

Our goal is not the victory of might, but the vindication of right—not peace at the expense of freedom, but both peace *and* freedom, here in this hemisphere, and, we hope, around the world. God willing, that goal will be achieved.

Thank you and good night.

Robert F. Kennedy

THE QUARANTINE DECISION

Robert F. Kennedy was a member of the Executive Committee, a special task force assembled to discuss possible U.S. alternatives in dealing with the Soviet installation of nuclear missiles in Cuba. In the following selection, published after Senator Kennedy's death in 1968, Kennedy relates how the decision to impose a quarantine took precedence over the alternative of an immediate military attack.

IT was during the afternoon and evening of that first day, Tuesday, [October 16, 1962] that we began to discuss the idea of a quarantine or blockade. Secretary McNamara, by Wednesday, became the blockade's strongest advocate. He argued that it was limited pressure, which could be increased as the circumstances warranted. Further, it was dramatic and forceful pressure, which would be understood yet, most importantly, still leave us in control of events. Later he reinforced his position by reporting that a surprise air strike against the missile bases alone—a surgical air strike, as it came to be called—was mil-

Reprinted from *Thirteen Days, A Memoir of the Cuban Missile Crisis* by Robert F. Kennedy by permission of W. W. Norton & Company, Inc. Copyright © 1969 by W. W. Norton & Company, Inc. Copyright © 1968 by McCall Corporation.

itarily impractical in the view of the Joint Chiefs of Staff, that any such military action would have to include all military installations in Cuba, eventually leading to an invasion. Perhaps we would come to that, he argued. Perhaps that course of action would turn out to be inevitable. "But let's not start with that course," if by chance that kind of confrontation with Cuba, and of necessity with the Soviet Union, could be avoided.

Those who argued for the military strike instead of a blockade pointed out that a blockade would not in fact remove the missiles and would not even stop the work from going ahead on the missile sites themselves. The missiles were already in Cuba, and all we would be doing with a blockade would be "closing the door after the horse had left the barn." Further, they argued, we would be bringing about a confrontation with the Soviet Union by stopping their ships, when we should be concentrating on Cuba and Castro.

Their most forceful argument was that our installation of a blockade around Cuba invited the Russians to do the same to Berlin. If we demanded the removal of missiles from Cuba as the price for lifting our blockade, they would demand the removal of missiles surrounding the Soviet Union as the reciprocal act.

And so we argued, and so we disagreed—all dedicated, intelligent men, disagreeing and fighting about the future of their country, and of mankind. Meanwhile, time was slowly running out.

An examination of photography taken on Wednesday, the 17th of October, showed several other installations, with at least sixteen and possibly thirty-two missiles of over a thousand-mile range. Our military experts advised that these missiles could be in operation within a week. The next day, Thursday, estimates by our Intelligence Community placed in Cuba missiles with an atomic-warhead potential of about one half the current ICBM capacity of the entire Soviet Union. The photography having indicated that the missiles were being directed at certain American cities, the estimate was that within a few minutes of their being

fired eighty million Americans would be dead.

The members of the Joint Chiefs of Staff were unanimous in calling for immediate military action. They forcefully presented their view that the blockade would not be effective. General Curtis LeMay, Air Force Chief of Staff, argued strongly with the President that a military attack was essential. When the President questioned what the response of the Russians might be, General LeMay assured him there would be no reaction. President Kennedy was skeptical. "They, no more than we, can let these things go by without doing something. They can't, after all their statements, permit us to take out their missiles, kill a lot of Russians, and then do nothing. If they don't take action in Cuba, they certainly will in Berlin."

The President went on to say that he recognized the validity of the arguments made by the Joint Chiefs, the danger that more and more missiles would be placed in Cuba, and the likelihood, if we did nothing, that the Russians would move on Berlin and in other areas of the world, feeling the U.S. was completely impotent. Then it would be too late to do anything in Cuba, for by that time all their missiles would be operational.

General David M. Shoup, Commandant of the Marine Corps, summed up everyone's feelings: "You are in a pretty bad fix, Mr. President." The President answered quickly, "You are in it with me." Everyone laughed, and, with no final decision, the meeting adjourned.

Later, Secretary McNamara, although he told the President he disagreed with the Joint Chiefs and favored a blockade rather than an attack, informed him that the necessary planes, men, and ammunition were being deployed and that we could be ready to move with the necessary air bombardments on Tuesday, October 23, if that was to be the decision. The plans called for an initial attack, consisting of five hundred sorties, striking all military targets, including the missile sites, airfields, ports, and gun emplacements.

I supported McNamara's position in

favor of a blockade. This was not from a deep conviction that it would be a successful course of action, but a feeling that it had more flexibility and fewer liabilities than a military attack. Most importantly, like others, I could not accept the idea that the United States would rain bombs on Cuba, killing thousands and thousands of civilians in a surprise attack. Maybe the alternatives were not very palatable, but I simply did not see how we could accept that course of action for our country.

Former Secretary of State Dean Acheson began attending our meetings, and he was strongly in favor of an air attack. I was a great admirer of his. In 1961, President Kennedy asked him to prepare a report for the National Security Council recommending a course of action to deal with the Russian threat to Berlin. Listening to his presentation then, I had thought to myself that I had never heard anyone so lucid and convincing and would never wish to be on the other side of an argument with him. Now he made his arguments that an air attack and invasion represented our only alternative in the same clear and brilliant way. He said that the President of the United States had the responsibility for the security of the people of the United States and of the whole free world, that it was his obligation to take the only action which could protect that security, and that that meant destroying the missiles.

With some trepidation, I argued that, whatever validity the military and political arguments were for an attack in preference to a blockade, America's traditions and history would not permit such a course of action. Whatever military reasons he and others could marshal, they were nevertheless, in the last analysis, advocating a surprise attack by a very large nation against a very small one. This, I said, could not be undertaken by the U.S. if we were to maintain our moral position at home and around the globe. Our struggle against Communism throughout the world was far more than physical survival—it had as its essence our heritage and our ideals, and these we must not destroy.

We spent more time on this moral question during the first five days than on any other single matter. At various times, it was proposed that we send a letter to Khrushchev twenty-four hours before the bombardment was to begin, that we send a letter to Castro, that leaflets and pamphlets listing the targets be dropped over Cuba before the attack— all these ideas and more were abandoned for military or other reasons. We struggled and fought with one another and with our consciences, for it was a question that deeply troubled us all.

Adlai Stevenson, Mario Garcia-Inchaustegui, Valerian Zorin

THE MISSILE CRISIS DEBATE IN THE UNITED NATIONS

MR. Stevenson: In view of the transformation of Cuba into a base for offensive weapons of sudden mass destruction, the President of the United States announced on October 22 the initiation of a strict quarantine on all offensive military weapons under shipment to Cuba.

Recent developments in Cuba—the importation of the cold war into the heart of the Americas—constitute a threat to the peace of this hemisphere and of the world.

Seventeen years ago the representatives of 51 nations gathered in San Francisco to adopt the Charter of the United

From "Points from the Initial Statements of the U.S., Cuba, and U.S.S.R. to the Security Council," *United Nations Review,* IX (November, 1962), pp. 12–13, 78–84.

Nations. These nations solemnly resolved to band together in a great cooperative quest for world peace and world progress. The adventure of the United Nations held out to humanity the bright hope of a new world, a world securely founded on international peace, on national independence, on personal freedom, on respect for law, for social justice and betterment, and, in the words of the Charter, for "equal rights and self-determination of peoples."

*   *   *

. . . The United States remains committed to the principles of the United Nations and intends to defend them.

We are engaged today in a crucial test of those principles. Nearly four years ago a revolution took place on the island of Cuba. This revolution overthrew a hated dictatorship in the name of democratic freedom and social progress. Dr. Castro made explicit promises to the people of Cuba.

Many in my country and throughout the Americas sympathized with Dr. Castro's stated objectives. The United States Government offered immediate diplomatic recognition and stood ready to provide the revolutionary régime with economic assistance.

But a grim struggle was taking place within the revolutionary régime, between its democratic and its predominant communist wings—between those who overthrew Batista to bring freedom to Cuba, and those who overthrew Batista to bring Cuba to communism. In a few months the struggle was over. By the end of 1959, the communist party was the only party in Cuba permitted freedom of political action. By early 1960, the Castro régime was entering into intimate economic and political relations with the Soviet Union.

All these events took place months before the United States stopped buying Cuban sugar in the summer of 1960—and many more months before exactions upon our Embassy in Havana forced the suspension of diplomatic relations in December 1960.

As the communization of Cuba proceeded, more and more democratic Cubans, men who had fought for freedom in the front ranks, were forced into exile. They were eager to return to their homeland and to save their revolution from betrayal. In the spring of 1961, they tried to liberate their country, under the political leadership of Dr. Castro's first Prime Minister and of a Revolutionary Council composed without exception of men who had opposed Batista and backed the Revolution. The people and Government of the United States sympathized with these men, but, still forbearing, that Government refrained from direct intervention. It sent no American troops to Cuba.

In the year and a half since, Dr. Castro has continued the communization of his unfortunate country. The 1940 constitution was never restored. Elections were never held, and their promise was withdrawn. The Castro régime fastened on Cuba an iron system of repression. It eradicated human and civil rights. It openly transformed Cuba into a communist satellite and a police state. Whatever benefit this régime might have brought to Cuba has long since been cancelled out by the firing squads, the drumhead executions, the hunger and misery, the suppression of civil and political and cultural freedom.

Yet even these violations of human rights, even this dictatorship, would not, if kept within the confines of one country, constitute a direct threat to the peace and independence of other states. The threat lies rather in the submission of the Castro régime to the will of an aggressive foreign power. It lies in its readiness to break up the relations of confidence and cooperation among the good neighbors of this hemisphere, at a time when the Alliance for Progress—that vast effort to raise living standards for all peoples of the Americas—has given new hope to the inter-American system.

The issue of Cuba is not an issue of revolution, of reform, of socialism or of dictatorship.

The foremost objection of the states of the Americas to the Castro régime is that he has aided and abetted an invasion of this hemisphere—an invasion just at the time when the hemisphere is making a new and unprecedented effort for economic progress and social reform. Cuba has given the Soviet Union a bridgehead and staging area in this hemisphere; it has invited an extracontinental, antidemocratic and expansionist power into the bosom of the American family; it has made itself an accomplice in the communist enterprise of world dominion.

There are those who seek to equate the presence of Soviet bases in Cuba with the presence of NATO bases in parts of the world near the Soviet Union.

Missiles which help a country to defend its independence, which leave the political institutions of the recipient countries intact, which are not designed to subvert the territorial integrity or political independence of other states, which are installed without concealment or deceit—assistance in this form and with these purposes is consistent with the principles of the United Nations. But missiles which introduce a nuclear threat into an area now free of it, which are installed by clandestine means, which result in the most formidable nuclear base in the world outside existing treaty systems—assistance in this form and with these purposes is radically different.

The missile sites in NATO countries were established in response to missile sites in the Soviet Union directed at the NATO countries. The NATO states had every right and necessity to respond to the installation of these Soviet missiles by installing missiles of their own. These missiles were designed to deter a process of expansion already in progress, and they have helped to do so.

The United States and its allies established their missile sites after free negotiation, without concealment and without false statements to other governments. There is a vast difference between the long-range missile sites established years ago in Europe and the long-range missile sites established by the Soviet Union in Cuba during the last three months.

There is a final significant difference. For 150 years the nations of the Americas have labored painfully to construct a hemisphere of independent and cooperating countries, free from foreign threats. An international system far older than the United Nations—the Inter-American System—has been erected on this principle. The principle of the territorial integrity of the Western hemisphere has been woven into the history, the life and the thought of all the people of the Americas. In striking at that principle, the Soviet Union is striking at the strongest and most enduring strain in the policy of this hemisphere. It is disrupting the convictions and aspirations of a century and a half. It is intruding on the firm policies of 20 nations. To allow this challenge to go unanswered would be to undermine a basic and historic pillar of the security of this hemisphere. . . .

Mr. García-Inchaústegui: Primarily because they are false and also because they are interventionist, Cuba rejects Mr. Stevenson's affirmations and statements regarding its history and social system.

When the representative of the United States referred to Cuba as "this once peaceful island," he was referring to the island of American investments, of racial discrimination, of exploitation and of illiteracy, to the island of the bloody dictatorship of Batista supported and armed by the Government of the United States. That island has disappeared forever, and it will never reappear, however many armadas the aggressive United States Government may send to its coasts.

Today direct war on the part of American imperialism hangs over our homeland more heavily than ever. We belong to a people that is ready to die for its independence and its sovereignty. And those of us who are ready to die have the inalienable right to have our words and voices heard by those who are pushing mankind to the holocaust.

We reject as false and dishonest all the accusations levelled by the President of the United States and repeated here by his representative.

The people and Government of Cuba have been forced to arm to defend themselves against the repeated aggressions of the United States Government, as Mr. [Osvaldo] Dorticós, President of Cuba, stated when he addressed the General Assembly recently.

The people of Cuba want peace; they do not want war. They have only one desire—to achieve great conquests in the development of their nation's future, but to do so by peaceful work, by creative labor. . . .

The United States has charged that our defensive arms affect the security of its territory. Are not the military potential and the aggressions of the North Americans a threat to our people? The idea that the Americans have of the juridical equality of states, which is set forth in Article 2, paragraph 1, of the Charter of the United Nations, is that the United States, as a military power, as a developed country, can promote, stimulate and carry out all types of aggressions, boycotts, sabotage, and all acts contrary to international law—and Cuba, a small but nevertheless courageous country, cannot arm in its own defence.

After the consecration of such a violation of law, what small country could be secure in its independence and sovereignty? It would suffice for a great neighboring power to decide that the system of any small state is a subversive system, or that its defences are a threat to security, for intervention and acts of war immediately to take place, such as those from which my country is suffering today. There would be no sovereignty left unscathed, and only the law of the strongest would prevail in relations between states.

Who are these who accuse Cuba of being a threatening base against United States territory? Those who possess the only foreign base in Cuba, against the will of our people, and those who now reinforce it so that from that base, too, they can attack us. It is those who have soldiers in every corner of the world, thousands of miles from their own territory. It is those who occupy Formosa, South Korea, who intervene in South Viet-Nam, who help the colonialists of Angola, and who have backed and continue to back the interventionist maneuvers in the Congo.

Obviously the Government of the United States reserves the right to determine when a rocket is good and when a rocket is naughty, when a base is good and when a base is naughty.

Hardly a week ago, when war hysteria against Cuba began among the United States Congressmen, Mr. Kennedy recognized publicly that the Cuban weapons were defensive. Now, and because his intelligence service informs him of it, he pushes the world to the brink of war without presenting proof of his statements, without even consulting his military allies. The United States sent its ships and its planes to and around Cuba, and then consulted its allies and the international organizations. From now on, war or peace—the ghastly nuclear war—will depend on what the United States intelligence service may deem it fit to affirm. It is as though international organizations and the Security Council have no reason to exist, as though any state could unilaterally assume the right to decide when certain measures affect its security.

What right does one member of the Organization have to insult and attack another member state because of its social system? The United Nations was born of the common effort of many states, with different social systems, in their struggle against nazi and fascist intolerance. What is the difference between the threats and aggressions of Hitler against his victims and the present aggressions of the United States against Cuba because of its social system?

What does it mean that our system is not negotiable in this hemisphere, and what type of morality is it that guides a government to negotiate with systems in accordance with their geographical locations? What contempt for the principles of the Charter—a Charter signed by states enjoying different social systems—is inherent in such practices? The Charter imposes peaceful negotiation on states in the settlement of their disputes. Cuba has always been ready to carry out peaceful negotiations and to seek a peaceful settlement of its conflict with the United States. The North American reply has been the haughty reply of one who tries to impose might over the law.

What the United States has done is to adopt a unilateral measure of war, based on its thirst for domination and neo-colonialist control—that is what the naval blockade of Cuba adds up to—and then to convoke the Security Council and other international bodies, with the idea of having them confirm its flagrant violation of law through pressures of all kinds.

To what international organization did the United States turn before the event, to inform it of the aggressive intent of the United States? Why did it not accuse Cuba before this Council and await the decision of the Council? The United States did not do so because it does not have one legal or moral reason upon which to base its measures of force taken against our country—measures of force which hurl the world to the brink of nuclear war and extermination.

What right has the United States to ask for dismantling and disarmament when it occupies a base in Cuba against the will of our own people and possesses all over the world aggressive bases against member states of this Organization? What basis has the United States for asking that observers should go to Cuba? Logically, United Nations observers should be sent to the United States bases from which invaders and pirates emerge to punish and harass a small state, whose only crime is that of struggling for the development of its own people. We will not accept any kind of observers in matters which fall within our domestic jurisdiction. The imperialistic manoeuvres in the Congo will not be repeated in Cuba.

The United States, which did not denounce Cuba to this international organization, did take measures without the consent of the Organization and has no right whatever to expect a blessing from the Organization on its violation of the law. Such a blessing or endorsement would be a shameful page in the annals of this Organization; it would be the very

seed of its destruction and the destruction of all mankind.

The United Nations must halt the arrogant intimidation that is being exercised over it by the United States. Either the United Nations will stop the United States in its headlong use of force, or the United States will destroy the United Nations and begin the extermination of thousands of people, including thousands of North Americans.

The naval blockade unilateral[ly] decreed by the United States is an act of war against the sovereignty and independence of our country, and it is a measure that our people will resist by all means in all ways. It is a desperate act on the part of the United States Government. It failed in all its efforts to destroy our revolution; now it is taking its last stand—war, although this may endanger the lives of thousands of people all over the world. The United States sent saboteurs to our country, and failed; it sent invasions to our country, and failed. The United States felt that, by means of economic boycott and other pressures, other countries would not trade with Cuba and that thus we might be besieged and finished by famine. But once again the United States failed. We would not bow to hunger.

What could the United States do then to reach an agreement with Cuba? For the peace of the world, we wish it had done so. The Charter imposes on member states the duty of settling their controversies peacefully and of refraining from the threat or use of force, but in the mind of the United States this applies to the powerful nations, to those possessing nuclear weapons, but not to Cuba, a small country a mere 90 miles from the empire.

Cuba has shaken off forever the shackles of the "sphere of influence." Cuba has ceased forever to belong to that area referred to by Mr. Kennedy as "well known because of its historic and special relations with the United States." Cuba is in Latin America, the Latin America of Rodó and Martí, the Latin America of Benito Juárez and of the heirs of Chapultepec. The history of the relations of the United States with the Latin American community during the last 150 years is a history of pillage and depredation, of violence and intervention, of confiscation of territory and of domination unequalled by any empire in the history of humanity.

This America of ours, the America of Martí, has as its northern limits the River Bravo. Cuba is a territory free of all Yankee interventionist influence and is a member of that Latin American community.

Finally, the United States calls on the Soviet Union to discuss with it the Cuban question. Does the United States not realize that the majority of the states of the world respect Cuba and that, among those states which respect Cuban sovereignty, is the Soviet Union? The relations between Cuba and other states are based on equality and on respect for the sovereignty of all. Cuba alone has the right to discuss and to decide upon its disputes with other states—the United States among them.

The American blockade against our country is an act of war. It is use of force by a great power against the independence of our home. It is a criminal act violating the Charter and the Principles of our Organization. We shall resist those illegal measures of North American imperialism. The reply of our people and our Government to the imminent armed attack of the United States has been general mobilization. . . .

Mr. Zorin: The statement by Mr. Stevenson betokens the total helplessness of the Government of the United States to defend its position in the face of the Council and of world public opinion.

He gave a falsified account of the history of postwar relations and has represented the whole position of the United States as being beneficent. He has tried to denigrate in every means possible the position of the Soviet Union. He has spoken of the history of the Cuban Revolution and has drawn an idyllic picture of the history of the Western Hemisphere during the past 150 years, but he seemed to have overlooked the policy of the "big stick" which now again the United States is trying to carry out.

On the question of bases in various parts of the world, he failed to mention that the United States, appropriating to itself the role of world policeman, has bases in 35 countries.

Mr. Stevenson has said practically nothing about the political, legal and moral grounds, based on the United Nations Charter, for those aggressive acts that were undertaken by the United States Government during the past 24 hours against the small Cuban state.

The Government of the United States has nothing to say in defence of its aggressive position. In the eyes of the entire world and of this Council, Mr. Stevenson stood here as the representative of an aggressive American brand of imperialism which rattles the sabre and demands that its own order be set up in the Western Hemisphere and throughout the world.

The Security Council has convened today in circumstances which can but give rise to the gravest concern for the fate of peace in the Caribbean region and in the whole world. The matter involved is unilateral and arbitrary action by a great power which constitutes a direct infringement of the freedom and independence of a small country. This involves a new and extremely dangerous act of aggression in a chain of such acts committed earlier by the United States against Cuba. It involves the violation of the most elementary rules and principles of international law, the violation of the fundamental provisions of the Charter and of the spirit and letter of that Charter.

Yesterday the United States in fact instituted a naval blockade of the Republic of Cuba, thus trampling underfoot the norms of international behavior and the principles enshrined in the Charter. The United States has appropriated to itself the right to attack ships of other countries on the open seas, and this constitutes nothing other than undisguised piracy.

At the same time, at the Guantánamo base on the territory of Cuba, landings of additional troops have been effected, and the armed forces of the United States brought to combat readiness. Such venturesome enterprises, together with the statements of the President of the United States to explain them, give evidence that American imperialist circles will balk at nothing in their attempts to throttle a sovereign state, a member of the United Nations. They are prepared, for the sake of this, to push the world to the brink of a military catastrophe.

Taking into account the great seriousness of the situation created by the Government of the United States, the Government of the Soviet Union published today, October 23, a special statement, warning the United States Government, that, "in carrying out the measures announced by President Kennedy, it is taking on itself a heavy responsibility for the fate of the world, and recklessly playing with fire." The Soviet Government also asked for the immediate convening of the Security Council to consider the violation of the Charter and the threat to peace by the United States. . . .

The Soviet delegation officially confirms the statement already made by the Soviet Union that the Soviet Government has not directed and is not directing to Cuba any offensive armaments. TASS of September 11, on the instructions of the Soviet Government, stated that the armaments and military *matériel* sent to Cuba was designed exclusively for defensive purposes. The Soviet Union did not need to relocate in any other country—for instance, in Cuba—the means available to it for repelling aggression and for a retaliatory blow. TASS added that the Soviet Union had so powerful a series of rockets and missile carriers that there was no need to seek a location for their launching anywhere outside the territory of the Soviet Union.

Observers of the United States in the Pacific recently were able to be convinced of the accuracy of the firing of Soviet rockets.

The Soviet Minister for Foreign Affairs, Mr. Gromyko, said in the General Assembly on September 21, that Cuba was not building up her forces to such a degree that she could pose a threat to the United States or to the passage of the United States to the Panama Canal, or else a threat to any state of the Western Hemisphere, and that the aid rendered by the Soviet Union to Cuba to strengthen her independence did not pursue any of those goals either.

The President of the Republic of Cuba, Mr. Osvaldo Dorticós, said in the General Assembly on October 8 that Cuba was forced to arm, not to attack anyone, but to defend itself; that it had never harbored any aggressive intentions against any nation of the continent.

And the Soviet Government's official statement now circulated to members of the Council once again declared that the Soviet Union's assistance to Cuba was exclusively designed to improve Cuba's defensive capacity. The Soviet Government had responded to the Cuban Government's request to help Cuba with arms intended solely for defensive purposes. Such assistance was necessitated by the fact that, from the outset of its existence, the Republic of Cuba had been subjected to continuous threats and acts of provocation by the United States.

The declaring of a naval blockade of Cuba and all those military measures that have been put into effect on the instructions of the President of the United States since yesterday—are they not threats or use of force against the territorial integrity or political independence of Cuba?

The United States is now trying to utilize fabrications in the Security Council for horrendous purposes and in order to try to compel the Security Council to approve retroactively those unlawful, aggressive actions of the United States which have already been adopted against Cuba, and which the United States is carrying out unilaterally, in clear violation of the Charter and of the elementary norms and principles of international law. The peoples of the world, however, must have a clear idea of the fact that in embarking upon an open adventure of this kind, the United States is taking a step toward the unleashing of a world thermonuclear war. This is the great terrible price which the world may have to pay for the present reckless and irresponsible actions of the United States.

Why did the United States begin its new aggressive action in such haste, and why is it trying to pretend that it is appealing to the Security Council? The purpose is in fact to place the Security Council before the *fait accompli* of United States aggression, to apprise the Council of all this simply for the sake of appearances.

The United States unilaterally has declared the implementation of an actual blockade of Cuba by the United States. It has directed large-scale military forces not only to the Cuban area but to the very territory of Cuba, to the United States base at Guantánamo, and has ordered them to be in a state of combat readiness. It has officially stated that it intends not to limit itself to this, but to take further action against Cuba if and when it finds that necessary.

The principal aspect of the present reckless actions of the United States against Cuba lies in the fact that on the basis of official United States statements the Government of the United States is prepared to move to the direct unleashing of a world thermonuclear war for the purpose of achieving its aggressive designs against Cuba.

The peace-loving countries and peoples have for a long time now had fears that the reckless and aggressive policies of the United States with respect to Cuba might bring the world to the brink of catastrophe, as shown in the records of the recently completed general debate.

In declaring the introduction of a blockade against Cuba, the United States has committed an unprecedented step in relations between states between which there is no formal state of war.

It has placed under threat the shipping of many countries of the world, including shipping of its allies which do not agree with this reckless and dangerous policy.

It has launched a direct challenge at the United Nations, and to the Security Council as the principal organ responsible for the maintenance of international peace and security.

In stating its intention to draw into the implementation of its aggressive actions the Organization of American States, the United States is openly violating the prerogatives of the Security Council which alone can authorize enforcement measures.

Could the Security Council overlook the fact that the United States is openly installing the law of the jungle in international relations?

The Security Council would fail in its direct duty as the principal organ responsible for the maintenance of international peace and security if it were to ignore or overlook the aggressive actions of the United States.

In summary, the realistic facts facing the Security Council are:

The decision of the United States to stop and inspect the ships of other countries which are headed for the shores of Cuba leads to a great intensification of the tension in the international situation, and constitutes a step toward the unleashing of world thermonuclear war, because no self-respecting state will permit its shipping to be tampered with.

The United States is trying to distort the defence measures undertaken by the Cuban Government.

John F. Kennedy

MESSAGE TO CHAIRMAN KHRUSHCHEV CALLING
FOR REMOVAL OF SOVIET MISSILES FROM CUBA, OCTOBER 27, 1962

DEAR Mr. Chairman:
I have read your letter of October 26th with great care and welcomed the statement of your desire to seek a prompt solution to the problem. The first thing that needs to be done, however, is for work to cease on offensive missile bases in Cuba and for all weapons systems in Cuba capable of offensive use to be rendered inoperable, under effective United Nations arrangements.

Assuming this is done promptly, I have given my representatives in New York instructions that will permit them to work out this weekend—in cooperation with the Acting Secretary General and your representative—an arrangement for a permanent solution to the Cuban problem along the lines suggested in your letter of October 26th. As I read your letter, the key elements of your proposals —which seem generally acceptable as I understand them—are as follows:

1. You would agree to remove these weapons systems from Cuba under appropriate United Nations observation and supervision; and undertake, with suitable safeguards, to halt the further introduction of such weapons systems into Cuba.

2. We, on our part, would agree—upon the establishment of adequate arrangements through the United Nations to ensure the carrying out and continuation of these commitments—(a) to remove promptly the quarantine measures now in effect and (b) to give assurances against an invasion of Cuba. I am confident that other nations of the Western Hemisphere would be prepared to do likewise.

If you will give your representative similar instructions, there is no reason why we should not be able to complete these arrangements and announce them to the world within a couple of days. The effect of such a settlement on easing world tensions would enable us to work toward a more general arrangement regarding "other armaments," as proposed in your second letter which you made public. I would like to say again that the United States is very much interested in reducing tensions and halting the arms race; and if your letter signifies that you are prepared to discuss a detente affecting NATO and the Warsaw Pact, we are quite prepared to consider with our allies any useful proposals.

But the first ingredient, let me emphasize, is the cessation of work on missile sites in Cuba and measures to render such weapons inoperable, under effective international guarantees. The continuation of this threat, or a prolonging of this discussion concerning Cuba by linking these problems to the broader questions of European and world security, would surely lead to an intensification of the Cuban crisis and a grave risk to the peace of the world. For this reason I hope we can quickly agree along the lines outlined in this letter and in your letter of October 26th.

JOHN F. KENNEDY

NOTE: Chairman Khrushchev's letter of October 26 was not released by the White House.

From *Public Papers of the Presidents of the United States: John F. Kennedy, 1962* (Washington, 1963), pp. 813–814.

John F. Kennedy

MESSAGE IN REPLY TO A BROADCAST BY CHAIRMAN KHRUSHCHEV

ON THE CUBAN CRISIS, OCTOBER 28, 1962

DEAR Mr. Chairman:

I am replying at once to your broadcast message of October twenty-eight, even though the official text has not yet reached me, because of the great importance I attach to moving forward promptly to the settlement of the Cuban crisis. I think that you and I, with our heavy responsibilities for the maintenance of peace, were aware that developments were approaching a point where events could have become unmanageable. So I welcome this message and consider it an important contribution to peace.

The distinguished efforts of Acting Secretary General U Thant have greatly facilitated both our tasks. I consider my letter to you of October twenty-seventh and your reply of today as firm undertakings on the part of both our governments which should be promptly carried out. I hope that the necessary measures can at once be taken through the United Nations, as your message says, so that the United States in turn will be able to remove the quarantine measures now in effect. I have already made arrangements to report all these matters to the Organization of American States, whose members share a deep interest in a genuine peace in the Caribbean area.

You referred in your letter to a violation of your frontier by an American aircraft in the area of the Chukotskiy Peninsula. I have learned that this plane, without arms or photographic equipment, was engaged in an air sampling mission in connection with your nuclear tests. Its course was direct from Eielson Air Force Base in Alaska to the North Pole and return. In turning south, the pilot made a serious navigational error which carried him over Soviet territory. He immediately made an emergency call on open radio for navigational assistance and was guided back to his home base by the most direct route. I regret this incident and will see to it that every precaution is taken to prevent recurrence.

Mr. Chairman, both of our countries have great unfinished tasks and I know that your people as well as those of the United States can ask for nothing better than to pursue them free from the fear of war. Modern science and technology have given us the possibility of making labor fruitful beyond anything that could have been dreamed of a few decades ago.

I agree with you that we must devote urgent attention to the problem of disarmament, as it relates to the whole world and also to critical areas. Perhaps now, as we step back from danger, we can together make real progress in this vital field. I think we should give priority to questions relating to the proliferation of nuclear weapons, on earth and in outer space, and to the great effort for a test ban. But we should also work hard to see if wider measures of disarmament can be agreed and put into operation at an early date. The United States Government will be prepared to discuss these questions urgently, and in a constructive spirit, at Geneva or elsewhere.

From *Public Papers of the Presidents of the United States: John F. Kennedy, 1962* (Washington, 1963), pp. 814–815.

III. THE UNITED STATES, CASTROISM, AND THE COLD WAR

William A. Williams

THE U.S., CUBA, AND CASTRO

Numerous critics of U.S. policy in Latin America argue that Cuba is a classic example of American failure to comprehend revolutionary nationalism in an emerging state. One exponent of this view, William A. Williams, a provocative diplomatic historian, contends that the United States compelled Castro to turn to Marxism and the Soviet Union.

THE United States quickly interpreted Castro's actions of late 1959, and his trade deal with the Soviet Union early in 1960, as meaning that Cuba had become a totalitarian Communist satellite. Most commentators have followed that official government line. Neither claim is factually correct. But the ideology which provided that simple, arbitrary explanation of a very complex reality is nevertheless important because it also produced the counter-revolutionary invasion of Cuba in April, 1961, almost 63 years to the day after the United States went to war to pacify Cuba in 1898.

It appears very probable, indeed, that the CIA began before the end of 1959 to work with counter-revolutionary groups in Cuba. This activity increased throughout 1960 and into the first months of 1961. Along the way, it involved active American military support in providing air cover for the smuggling of arms and other supplies to Castro's enemies in Cuba. The formal American decision to arm and train an exile army, however, was not made until March, 1960.

This chronology of its Cuban operations, along with a great deal of other evidence, makes it perfectly clear that it is the CIA—rather than the military—which functions as an independent variable in the formulation and conduct of American foreign policy. The military does have great influence, both directly within the government and indirectly through its ties with the industrial complex of the country. Civilians gave the military such influence by defining the world in military terms (both in 1939 and again in 1945), but the military cannot independently conceive and mount an operation having immediate and profound effects on foreign policy.

The CIA not only *can* do that, it *has done* it a good many times. The CIA has originated projects, persuaded the President and other high officials to authorize them on the basis of information provided by the CIA, and then executed the operation through its own agents. It is a self-validating civilian agency with vast areas of independent action in foreign policy. And it was created and is sustained by civilians.

The real points at issue in all this do not concern the wearing of uniforms after being graduated and commissioned from one of the service academies. The questions involve the far more important matters of how one explains America's difficulties and defines its opportunities, and whether or not one is willing to resort to force in solving the problems or ex-

From William A. Williams, *The U.S., Cuba, and Castro: An Essay in the Dynamics of Revolution and the Dissolution of Empire* (New York, 1962), pp. 139–148, 156–161, 163–171. Reprinted by permission of Monthly Review Press. Copyright © 1962 by William Appleman Williams.

ploiting the openings. These subjects are crucial to an understanding of the invasion of Cuba.

The American propensity to externalize evil is at least as well developed as any known to history. We have followed that self-righteous path of least resistance since we won our independence. It is wholly unnecessary to dwell either on the extent or the intensity of the manner in which American leaders and the public at large have done this with reference to the Soviet Union. What is not so generally recognized, however, is the degree to which Americans have also externalized good. The extent, that is, to which they have argued (and finally assumed) that America's political and economic well-being are determined by opportunities that exist outside the United States. This began at least as early as Jefferson's reliance on the frontier to underwrite prosperity and representative government, and has continued to the present day. Americans have always relied on a new frontier.

The United States has furthermore exhibited a pronounced tendency to deal with its difficulties, and to exploit its opportunities, through the use (or the threat) of economic or political force. A rudimentary listing of our wars, quasi-wars, police actions, and interventions makes the point. We have fought, in rough order (and counting only the first conflicts since there are several repeaters), the following nations: various Indian tribes that *we* defined as independent societies, England, France, Spain, Canada, Mexico, Nicaragua, Hawaii, China, Colombia, Germany, Austria-Hungary, various other Latin American governments, Japan, Italy, several Eastern European countries, Koreans, and sundry other Asians. We have applied strong—even massive—economic force as a conscious instrument of policy to every nation with which we have ever had significant relations. None of this makes us unique. Other major powers have their own lists. But that is just the point. We are not unique.

These features of American thought and action in foreign affairs have characterized the policy of the United States toward Cuba not only since 1895, but in particular since Senator [Wayne] Morse's warning to the Cubans on January 12, 1959. By the end of that year, the two official notes on the Agrarian Reform Law (along with many others concerning American property rights), and the increasing agitation to discipline Castro (evil) and thereby re-open Cuba to American influence (good), made it clear that the traditional outlook was as dominant as ever.

On November 29, 1959, for example, Senator [Allen] Ellender fired another volley on the sugar quota issue. A bit later, on December 10, Secretary of State Christian Herter made it known that Castro's offer on compensation for American property was no more acceptable than the earlier and similar Guatemalan proposal. And as the Congress reconvened in January, 1960, a consensus began to emerge very rapidly around the idea, as one Representative put it, that "this is a time for action and not pussy-footing."

The outcry that greeted Cuba's barter deal with the Russians in February, 1960, could have been predicted. This bargain was largely the result of three factors. First, Castro's serious economic problems. Second, America's refusal to help solve those difficulties save in a way that would subvert the Revolution. And third, the not particularly astute realization by the Soviets that they could exploit those two conditions in a way that might bring them significant gains. American policy—long-run and short term—handed the Russians an opening which they promptly exploited. The United States had both the power and the opportunity to avoid that situation. It did not do so.

The greatest gain that Russia ultimately won from its decision to aid Castro concerned the opportunity it finally secured to sit in on the game that the United States had been playing ever since 1945. Moscow could at last talk about its ally on the border of the United States. And it unquestionably began to use Cuba, as it already used other Latin American countries, as a center for the distribution of propaganda and as a base for intelligence operations.

But there was in 1960, and as of September, 1962, there still is, a vital difference. The Russians did not establish Soviet bases in Cuba as the United States has done in such nations as Turkey along the frontiers of the Soviet Union. Moscow constructed no airfields to handle Red Air Force bombers armed with nuclear weapons, built no launching pads for Soviet missiles tipped with hydrogen warheads, and flew no U-2 flights over the United States from Cuba.

The Russians were quite aware of this difference: they understand, even though many Americans seem not to, that their link with Cuba has not changed the essential balance of power which stands in favor of the United States.

American reaction to the Castro-Soviet trade agreement, and to the subsequent development of the tie between the two countries, seems to have been based on the same assumption that produced the policy of containment vis-à-vis the Soviet Union—only this time applied to the United States instead of Russia. It appears to have been grounded, that is, on the axiom that the United States could not continue to exist as a democratic and prosperous capitalist nation if any major European power challenged or blocked or decreased its existing power in, or its potential expansion into, areas and countries along its frontiers.

In any event, President Eisenhower's first response was to approve the proposal to arm and train Cuban counter-revolutionaries. The United States next refused to sell helicopters to Castro. Then, on April 20, 1960, the House of Representatives passed a law prohibiting aid to Castro unless a special finding was made to define and authorize such assistance as being in the interests of the United States. The Cubans seem to have interpreted this last act for what it was —the beginning of the shift from letting Castro "go through the wringer" to a policy of speeding up the process. In any event, the revolutionary government made overtures in May to discuss the deteriorating situation.

The United States declined the offer. Instead, on May 26, 1960, it cancelled all aid programs then in operation. This assistance did not amount to very much, but the move indicated how rapidly America was moving to increase its pressure on Castro. Exactly a month later, the House Committee on Agriculture granted the President power to fix the Cuban sugar quota.

After that act, if not indeed from February, the record of American-Cuban relations reads like the script for a crude burlesque on the action-reaction, vicious-circle kind of diplomacy. Castro next seized the Texaco and Esso refineries for refusing to process Soviet crude petroleum. The American note of protest was strong, inaccurate, rather emotional, and filled with portents of retaliation.

That came from both sides on July 6, 1960. Cuba announced Revolutionary Law 851, which established the legal basis for the general nationalization of American and Cuban property. Seizures under the law began almost immediately and continued throughout the year. For its part, the United States reduced the Cuban sugar quota by 700,000 short tons. A bit later, on July 16, it filed "a most solemn and serious protest" against Law 851. It asserted, contrary to the careful opinions of Cuba's best lawyers (given in response to the inquiries of American business interests), that the legislation was "manifestly in violation" of international law. The State Department argument was in essence the same one that had been used in connection with the Agrarian Reform Law. Cuba's action was illegal because it failed "to assure the payment of prompt, adequate, and effective compensation." Despite the grave tone of the American note, Cuba did not rescind the law.

Similar rounds of tit-for-tat continued throughout the summer. And the reality of such clashes was to some extent infused with the kind of mounting anger and small-boy behavior generally associated with the game. The specific timing and tone of some of the exchanges, for example, were undoubtedly guided by that spirit of dare and double-dare. But it is a mistake to *explain* the diplomacy in those terms. Each side had embarked upon a broad course of action which generated fundamental opposition from the other, and the details, timing, and tone of the incidents were secondary and derivative in nature.

It is at this point—*but not before*—that Meyer and Szulc* offer considerable insight in speaking of the tragic nature of American-Cuban relations. Tragedy is defined by the confrontation and clash of opposing truths. And there was truth on both sides. Cuba's truth involved the need for a thoroughgoing social revolution, the right to carry it through, and the legitimate expectation that its former overlord would either help ease the transition or leave it alone to proceed as it could and would on its own. The American truth involved past concern and assistance, existing rights and economic stakes in Cuba per se, and the legitimate expectation that the Revolution would make its transition with consideration for those American equities.

There is, as Meyer and Szulc explain, the element of inevitability inherent in the concept of tragedy. The conflict between such clashing truths will produce disaster if neither of the protagonists breaks into and changes the logic of the confrontation. But Meyer and Szulc are mistaken on two important counts. The element of inevitability which they stress is always conditional until *after* the tragedy materializes. *The concept of tragedy is a means of explaining something that has happened.* It does not account for the actual events save in and to the degree that the actors entertain and act upon a tragic outlook. And neither Castro nor American policy-makers were men of that nature. The inevitability that Meyer and Szulc emphasize was *not* present from the outset.

But if we accept the broad conceptual approach of thinking about American-Cuban relations within the framework of tragedy—but abandon the theme of inevitability—then we are able to see and raise the central questions. These concern which protagonist had the greater responsibility for acting to change the tragic logic, and what men made the effort.

* Karl E. Meyer and Tad Szulc, *The Cuban Invasion: Chronicle of a Disaster* (New York, 1962). [Editor's note.]

The United States had the vastly greater responsibility. It took control of Cuban affairs in the period between 1895 and 1902 and never relinquished its final authority. In addition, it asserted and preened itself on a morality which required it to use that power in ways that would have avoided the conditions of the Cuban political economy in 1958, and which would have led to a different approach to the Revolution of 1959 once it had occurred. By its own actions and its proclaimed morality, therefore, the burden was on the United States.

American policy did not measure up to those responsibilities between 1895 and 1959, or between January, 1959, and the opening of the presidential election campaign in August, 1960. It is conceivable that, without the added pressure and competitive bidding inherent in such a campaign, relations between the United States and Cuba would have continued to be critically difficult without culminating in an invasion. Not only conceivable, but actually rather probable. Formal relations might even have been broken, for example, without leading to such an attack. That kind of temporary hiatus had developed a good many times in the history of American foreign relations.

There are two general reasons for questioning the assumption (or the argument) that things would have worked out as they did even had there been no election campaign. The first of these involves a negative consideration. It may very seriously be doubted that President Eisenhower would ever have given the go-ahead signal for the invasion of Cuba. It is true that he authorized the organization and training of an exile force. But he did so very reluctantly, and that action did not commit him to an invasion.

The decision to launch such an assault would have cut across several of Eisenhower's most central character traits. Behind the militant, extremist, and self-righteous rhetoric of Secretary of State [John Foster] Dulles, which attracted most of the attention and comment, stood Eisenhower's far calmer temperament and his deep disinclination to involve the United States in action that violated what he considered to be America's moral integrity. He was a man more concerned with the way power was used than either with its use or merely retaining it.

Eisenhower's stand against the British-French-Israeli invasion of Egypt is a typical example of this central feature of his outlook. He also had a deep aversion to becoming involved in combat operations that cost American lives. This is perhaps the most telling point of all. Let us assume that Eisenhower had come to the point of considering such an invasion of Cuba. Let us even assume that he had overcome his moral scruples against violating American law and the obligations of the United States involved in the treaty structure of the Organization of American States. Given those conditions, Eisenhower most assuredly—as a military officer with long experience in such command decisions—would never have considered allowing the operation to fail for want of overt American military action. But that very military realism would have collided with his deep reluctance to send Americans into another battle—and it seems very likely that the latter element would have triumphed.

The second negative factor involved in evaluating the role of the election campaign derives from Eisenhower's unhappy experience with the CIA. Despite his own recurrent doubts and uneasiness, he went along for four years with that organization's assurances concerning the U-2 flights over the Soviet Union. Then, in a dramatic and never-to-be-forgotten failure, the program destroyed his last chance of achieving his most treasured goal—the working out of an understanding with Russia that would open the way for lasting peace. It may therefore seriously be doubted that he would have relied upon the CIA in another major decision—particularly in view of his own temperament and values.

The positive factor related to questioning the inevitability of the invasion arises out of the role of American-Cuban relations in the election campaign, and from the essential character and outlook of the two candidates—and more particularly of the man who won. It seems probable that Richard Nixon would also have gone ahead with an invasion. After all, he had proposed training the exiles as early as April, 1959. And we now know that his seemingly fundamental attack on John F. Kennedy's Cuban policy during the campaign was a massive deception of the American people undertaken to preserve the pseudo-secrecy of the exile training program. It could be argued, of course, that Nixon would have cut free of the exiles once they were trained and ready. That seems very doubtful, if only because the dynamics of the campaign would have made it very difficult to risk the failure inherent in a policy of real laissez faire. And Eisenhower's influence would have been undercut by Nixon's need to be his own president—as well as by the not-so-latent tension between the two men.

* * *

What we have to do, if we are to avoid similar disasters in the future (and perhaps the very near future), is to face up to five specific lessons to be learned from our dealings with Cuba since 1895. This ought to be done now, however much we may prefer to avoid the unpleasantness involved, because we need to do so and because the time is short.

First. The lesson of United States responsibility.

This responsibility takes several forms of a general and specific nature. The United States instigated and fought to a successful conclusion the first modern revolution for independence from a colonial empire. We are, at least in this sense, the exemplar of the anti-colonial and anti-imperialist movement. We have pitted and tarnished that reputation by our actions throughout the world since at least as early as 1895, and by our conduct toward Cuba in particular, but the United States is still a model and an image of that kind of revolution. We have a clear moral obligation to support and assist such revolutions—even when they are staged against our power and influence. Indeed, particularly when they are waged against us.

This broad kind of responsibility also

exists in connection with the United States as an industrial nation of enormous power and wealth. We have consistently and insistently presented ourselves as *the* wonder of the modern world, whose goals and methods should be followed by all other societies. For that matter, we have often asserted that they must follow our example if they are to avoid the most terrible consequences. Considered in terms of either imperative thus offered the poor and developing countries—the moral or the logical—the United States has created for itself an obligation to facilitate the efforts of countries that manifest a desire to emulate its achievement.

These considerations are particularly relevant to the case of Cuba. The United States first took the island and controlled it as a colony, then placed it in a semicolonial condition, and finally created an economic relationship that accomplished the essential political and social as well as economic purposes of colonialism without the embarrassments and troublesome administrative problems connected with the traditional pattern. As an integral part of that relationship, moreover, the United States encouraged Cuba to think of its own future in terms of the American standard of living. The United States was not only responsible for the conditions that produced Castro, but for the broad objectives of the Revolution itself.

Finally, and in the narrower and more explicit sense, the United States bears the responsibility for two kinds of intervention against Castro's Revolution. It first chose not to help Castro except on its own, unilaterally determined, conditions. It refused to supply such assistance with a clear—even brilliant—understanding of the consequences that its decision would produce. Then the United States planned, financed, and directed a military action designed to destroy the Castro government and replace it with one extensively dependent upon American favor. In both cases, furthermore, the United States knew and accepted the fact that its action would bring additional death, pain, and suffering to the Cuban people. This grave responsibility cannot be mitigated by saying that no American combat units fired upon Cubans. That claim may actually be false. But even if it is valid, it remains true that American policy has caused—and continues to cause—death, pain, and suffering to the population of Cuba.

Second. The lesson that revolutions are dynamic, not static.

This seems in some respects to be the truth that most Americans have the greatest difficulty in grasping. One is constantly and ever more strongly impressed, in reading the newspaper and magazine accounts (and in reviewing oral commentary) on the Cuban Revolution, with the extent to which Americans assumed that the Revolution should—as well as would—end with the defeat of Batista. While it is too much to say that Americans were truly surprised by the idea of a revolution that aimed to change the old order, it is not too much to say that they were rapidly and increasingly perplexed and annoyed that the Cuban revolutionaries meant to make fundamental changes, and intended to go ahead with their program in the face of opposition and criticism.

One suspects, in the end, that this is one of the unfavorable results—one of the costs—of being first. It has been so long since we had a revolution that we are very much out of touch with that rudimentary feature of political and social reality. This is true even if one views the Civil War, at least in some respects, as a revolution. One hundred years—let alone two centuries—is a long time between revolutions. No other major country in the world has been tucked away in a cocoon for anything approaching that length of time. (England is *not* an exception because the British Empire has experienced many colonial uprisings which involved not only the politics—but also the people—of the British Isles.)

We seem to have forgotten, furthermore, some mundane but nevertheless essential features of our own revolutions. They lasted a long time (1774–1789, and 1860–1876); they were violent and bloody, and those who opposed them suffered great losses up to and including their lives; they were affected by the attitudes and policies of foreign countries; and some of the avowed objectives of the revolutions—such as the emancipation of the Negro—have still not been achieved. All of these considerations are directly relevant to our attitudes and behavior toward the Cuban Revolution. One has the distinct impression, for example, that most Americans considered it something of a personal affront as well as a general insult that the Cubans had the gall to take their politics so seriously. And we have judged and condemned the Revolution long before it is even completed—let alone before its fruits have blossomed and matured. It is like judging a child for life at the end of a particularly bad week during adolescence, and proceeding ever afterward to act upon that judgment.

Each of these features of a revolution could be examined in considerable detail. Perhaps it is time, for that matter, for some talented historian or social critic to reacquaint the American people with the facts of life about revolutions per se. To provide, as it were, a poverty-guns-and-ideas version of the birds-and-the-bees story. A simple, blunt book on that subject might have vastly more positive consequences for American foreign policy than all the explanations and analyses of Communism and foreign aid that have been written since 1945.

Such an undertaking is clearly beyond the scope of this essay, but it is necessary to discuss two characteristics of revolutions that have a particularly direct connection with American thought and action concerning Cuba and Castro. It is essential to understand, and to think and act in terms of, the truth that a revolution is not a struggle for desirable but deferrable fringe benefits. A revolution is a battle over and about and for the fundamental structure, substance, direction, and tone of the society itself. Revolutions are made by men who care deeply about basic issues and who are driven into action by their commitment.

Hence it is largely irrelevant to belabor them for caring so much that they refuse to give up the revolution either because we want them to in order to make our life less difficult, or because some of their actions contradict ideas or ideals they proclaim as part of the revolution. In the first place, most revolutionaries—and most certainly Castro among them—are intensely aware of this problem. Indeed, much of their wild rhetoric is produced by the tension that results from their awareness. An intense consciousness of the odds on failure is the very texture of their existence.

In the second place, it is childish—if not simply dishonest—to pretend for the purposes of making severe judgments as though fundamental changes can be brought about without painful costs. If one began, for example, with the year 1876 and added up all the deaths and other harsh and desperate human costs that it took to win—finally—the routine, functioning acceptance of unions, and the installation of safety devices, in either mining or railroading, one would discover that even non-revolutionary changes come at an extremely high price. Yet we in America have judged Castro as though the United States moved from the conditions of 1776 to those of 1962 through a process of joyful goodwill and immaculate rationality. The point of this lesson about revolutions is that the truly moral and intelligent objectives for outsiders involve help to reduce those costs to the lowest possible level—not demands that the revolution be abandoned, or sermons about evil men who refuse to give up their mistaken goals.

Another central feature of social revolutions is that they are made by coalitions. This means that conflict is built into the revolutionary government that takes power on the morrow of victory. Just such a coalition started and fought the American Revolution, and governed the new nation during the period from 1783 to 1786. By 1785, however, that coalition was dividing into rival blocs over the questions of policy toward the West and the need and desirability of a stronger central government. Violent personal antagonisms developed, extremist and abusive language became the vernacular of political debate, secession was seriously considered both in the North and the South, and at one point (in the 1790's) civil war seemed to many men a distinct probability.

A similar, and far more violent and embittered, conflict took place inside the Bolshevik Revolution. To think of Soviet politics as being monolithic is like thinking of the atom as being a teeny-weeny marble. The fight between Stalin and Trotsky was merely the most famous of such battles within Russia. In the middle 1920's, for example, a serious and extremely significant debate over the means and tempo of industrialization, and the way to handle the agricultural problem, engaged all elements of the Communist Party and set the pattern of Soviet development for two decades.

As these two disparate examples indicate, it is very misleading in two crucial respects to think about revolutions as being either wholly democratic or wholly non-democratic. Such a difference exists in theory, and it is approached in practice. But that either-or approach distorts reality by substituting a choice between abstract and polarized opposites for what is actually the problem of estimating the degree of representative government, and of evaluating the direction and momentum toward or away from that objective. This judgment has to be made, furthermore, in terms of a revolution—not in terms of evolutionary changes occurring within a fundamentally stable framework.

* * *

Third. The lesson that we live in a volatile world in which most of the revolutions are occurring in societies which lack a powerful middle class.

This means, in the first place, that any effort to encourage and support middle-class revolutions amounts to an artificial forcing of history. That can be done—if at all—only through the direct and sustained use of force. To put it bluntly, such middle-class revolutions are minority revolutions which have no general basis of power in the poor society itself,

and hence have to be assisted and supported by American power.

It also means, and this is often overlooked, that the forcing of such middle-class revolutions upon a society not ready for them tends to increase the probability, and to accelerate the time table, of a lower-class revolution which will be even more radical and more violent than if it came to power at the present time. It is this consideration which gives meaning to the paradoxical remark, put most neatly by Herbert L. Matthews of the *New York Times*, that the most fortunate thing about the American invasion of Cuba was that it failed. Had it succeeded in establishing a middle-class group in power, the result would have been either a prolonged period of American armed intervention or a truly orgiastic upheaval against the American-installed government.

Finally, the propensity to think and act in terms of middle-class revolutions is very apt to produce extremely frustrating results. The assumption is, of course, that such revolutions will usher in a period of stability, of law and order, and of pro-Americanism. But premature middle-class revolutions are inherently unstable. For one thing, control of the government becomes the object of a contest between the elites in command of the various functional segments of the middle class. And the small operational base of the middle class invites upper-class coups and lower-class rebellions. Either of these developments may occur, as they are presently doing in Argentina, Brazil, and Venezuela. But, even if they do not (or if they are repressed), the middle class has to bid for support from its rivals. In any case, American expectations are seldom fulfilled.

All these considerations combine to suggest that the American choice lies between three alternatives: the United States can support upper-class, conservative revolutions, it can support and assist lower-class revolutions, or it can stay out of the situation and permit the various elements within the societies in question to proceed with their own struggles and revolutions in their own way. Whatever the decision on that matter, it cannot be made intelligently save in the context of the next lesson of the Cuban experience.

Fourth. The lesson that we cannot think intelligently or effectively about the present so long as we do so in terms of the past. One of the crucial values of studying history is that it helps us learn what to forget because it is irrelevant or misleading. Such things are of course part of history, and cannot be erased, but they do not provide significant insights into either the past or the present.

We cannot, that is to say, consider the option of supporting upper-class revolutions on the assumption that the upper class in poor and developing societies is comparable either with our own upper-class Founding Fathers, or with the best and most socially conscious and responsible of our existing leaders. The reason for this is simple: they are generally not comparable. This is not meant as a personal slur on any individuals. It is meant as a historical and sociological judgment. There are exceptions, but the basic proposition remains valid.

America's Founding Fathers were the product of two centuries of development involving a tradition of upper-class responsibility and training, and of an unparalleled opportunity to exploit the economic and political advantages of a fabulously wealthy continent separated from the seat of empire by 3,000 miles in an age of sailing vessels.

Upper-class leaders in Latin America, and in most other poor areas, have simply not enjoyed those remarkably favorable circumstances. Their original traditions of *noblesse oblige* have atrophied, and they have been watched over and controlled with all the efficiency of a world intimately bound together by instantaneous communications and highly mobile striking forces with great fire power. To support this group means to continue such controls while educating its members to modern standards of a socially conscious upper class. It would involve turning the government itself into a trade school modeled on Harvard, Annapolis, and the Chicago (or Wharton) School of Business. And that is a

project to think about very carefully and soberly before undertaking it.

Neither can the United States consider the alternative of supporting radical, lower-class revolutions as though it were a problem of repeating the New Deal in foreign lands while avoiding the participation of Communists. *We are simply not living in the 1930's any longer.*

To begin with, the New Deal did not solve any structural problems in the United States, and it is basically irrelevant to the conditions, circumstances, and aspirations of the poor countries at the present time. Those societies are struggling to throw off the vestiges of feudalism and colonialism, and to build the foundations and framework of an independent country with a balanced, dynamic political economy. The New Deal was an approach to saving and reforming a mature industrial capitalism. And it did not succeed by its own fundamental criteria of generating prosperity and social equity under conditions of peace. One would be far better off, at least in this rudimentary respect of finding an earlier model for the poor countries to emulate, to go back to the British mercantilists of the 17th and 18th centuries. Or to Americans of the period between 1785 and 1828. After all, Albert Gallatin and John Quincy Adams had Five Year Plans long before the Russians even had any Bolsheviks.

This might even be helpful in connection with the problem of evolving a mature attitude toward radical dissenters. The Puritans, who were in the beginning as doctrinaire, bigoted, and ruthless as the Communists of a later period, turned out to be extremely valuable mercantilists and state builders once they were accepted as members of the community. There is nothing quite as effective as exclusion to create and nourish extremism.

It is simply not true to say, as [Theodore] Draper and others do, that Communism and Communists do not change. They are changing all the time. If one really holds the view that Communists cannot and do not modify their thinking and change their programs, then there is really nothing to do but bury down in a shelter-centered garrison state and get it over with.

Nor will it do to call people "new" Communists, as Draper does, even though they are not actually Communists but only radicals collaborating with Communists inside a coalition. Or to refuse to draw a clear line between men who are inspired and guided by Marx but who are not Communists in terms of Stalin's Russia or Mao's China. This is to destroy even the *possibility* of supporting lower-class revolutions. And to destroy alternatives on false grounds is the height of anti-intellectualism. It is also to block off as being evil a policy that could very well open up an era of vast and exciting development within such poor and backward societies—and of much better relations with them. Yet that is precisely the result of thinking about radical lower-class revolutions in terms of the 1930's and the Soviet Union. It is a highly dangerous fixation shared by conservatives and liberals as well as ex-radicals.

Finally, it is very misleading to think about keeping our hands off the revolutions in the poorer countries as though that course involved a return to what is called isolationism. Since the United States has been actively involved in world affairs—has been a world power—ever since it broke away from the British Empire, it is very questionable whether the term isolationism has any usefulness whatsoever. If it has any meaning, however, it is in connection with the refusal of the United States to join the League of Nations in 1919, and with the reluctance of the nation to take strong action leading to war against the Axis Powers in the middle and later 1930's. Yet throughout that period from 1919 to 1941 the United States carried on a very active diplomacy in all parts of the world.

But even if we admit that such a specific and restricted definition of isolationism has some validity, it still has no relevance in connection with a discussion of the proper policy toward revolutions in underdeveloped countries in the second half of the century. The idea behind restraining oneself toward such revolutions does not even imply breaking off diplomatic relations, let alone ignoring the nation in question. It simply means allowing the society to have its revolution and then working out an appropriate relationship with the new society and its government. As far as the problem of the nationalization of American property is concerned, the American taxpayer is already paying for insurance to cover such crises.

This policy of restraint is the most demanding of all the possible approaches toward revolutions. This is true even in cases where the revolutions do not impinge upon the vital national interests of the United States. We are caught up in a pattern of thinking which externalizes good as well as evil. Hence we assume we have to control everything—events that do not threaten our welfare and safety just as well as those that do have a negative impact on our national interests.

The result is an inability to leave anything alone anywhere in the world. Internationalism has become intermeddling. We have defined our business as coterminous with every crossroad in the world. By that definition, minding one's own business becomes a process of minding the world. We are more than a little bit like the parent who cannot let go of the child as it approaches and crosses the threshold into adulthood. Such parents have lived vicariously through their children to the extent that letting the child go means giving up a major part of the meaning of their own adult life. We have defined so much of America in terms of the world that we are afraid to allow the world to develop in a pluralistic manner. Yet this is precisely what we must do if we are to retain any of our self-respect, and even any of our opportunity to build the kind of an America that we are capable of creating.

Indeed, we have been so busy thinking about the world that we have done very little thinking about the United States. And it shows in the state of the nation—and the society.

Fifth. The lesson that the place to begin is by changing our present policy toward Cuba. In a sense, of course, the act of changing policy is not a beginning, but a culmination; it represents a learning of the other, less explicit and visible, lessons that the history of American-Cuban relations offers for our consideration. History itself does not teach anything. History merely offers a way for people to learn by reflecting upon the record and the inter-relationships of what they have done. And learning of that kind is notably difficult because it involves both the admission that we have not always been intelligent or moral, and the will to adjust our behavior accordingly.

This lesson involving a change of policy is made still more demanding by the continuing changes in Cuba itself, and in the relationship between Cuba, the United States, and the Soviet Union. But neither American policy-makers nor the public at large can expect reality to stand still while they pull even with it at their leisure—or assume that one or two acts will stabilize or tranquilize the situation. Any significant change of policy involves a period of time during which the new approach seems to produce little or no improvement. The disappointments and frustrations of that period have to be understood and endured with patience and understanding; otherwise the reaction back toward a harsher version of the old policy will produce even more serious trouble.

The events of the spring and summer of 1962 serve to illustrate these difficulties. Castro's persistent efforts to strengthen the position of the 26th July Movement within its coalition with the Cuban Communists were dramatized early in the year by his effective attack on the Communist leader Aníbal Escalante. Escalante left the country, and others who had sympathized with or supported him also lost their positions. These developments coincided with a reassessment of the campaign to move Cubans into agricultural cooperatives and a decision to return some land to individual ownership and cultivation, and with renewed overtures by Castro for a rapprochement with the United States. His basic proposal, to negotiate compensation for American property that had been nationalized in return for renewed American sugar purchases, seems in fact to have been in the process of being con-

sidered by the State Department in June. But American policy-makers were not ready to act. Had they been, it seems possible that the opening might have led to a decrease in tension and a slow improvement of relations.

Such a rapprochement might have proceeded rapidly enough, if the United States had been prepared to move promptly, to have provided Castro and the Revolution with an alternate way of coping with their difficulties. These troubles were partly inherent in the development of the Revolution, partly the consequence of past and existing American policy, and partly the result of what many informed observers have called the worst drought in at least 40 years. Castro needed general and continuing economic assistance in reorganizing the Cuban economy and short-run aid to meet the immediate crisis. And, *so long as the United States did not give any firm indication that it was going to modify or change its policy*, Castro had to act on the assumption that he required more military support.

Given the failure of the United States to move quickly to meet his overtures, Castro turned again to the Soviet Union. The Russians began to pour in the help that he requested. In the short run, that only increased the tension. This took two forms. First, it made it increasingly difficult for Castro and other non-Communist Cuban radicals to maintain, let alone improve, their position vis-à-vis the Cuban Communists inside the government. American policy thus had the practical effect of subverting its own avowed objectives; or, at any rate, of making it ever more difficult to achieve those objectives short of a recourse to general violence. Secondly, the extremely militant reaction in the United States during September, 1962, recalled the similar outbursts of invasion talk during the fall of 1897 and the spring of 1898. Much of the rhetoric even sounded as though it had been lifted from the newspapers and the *Congressional Record* of that earlier period and reused after merely substituting Russia for Spain.

And it might be that the result, at least in some respects, would turn out to be similar. The United States might indeed invade Cuba in order to be done with Castro and the Revolution. It is misleading, however, to think solely in terms of such direct military intervention by American forces. The non-military pressure exerted by the United States on Castro and Cuban society has been and is enormous. It is wholly possible, for example, for the direct and indirect encouragement and assistance given Castro's opponents to create a grave crisis. The murder of Castro, to consider but one possibility, would very probably lead to a period of horrible violence and destruction. Whether the Cuban Communists won out, or whether some anti-Castro coalition emerged victorious, the cost paid by Cuban society would be immense. Even the latter result, while superficially a triumph for American policy, would of necessity involve the United States in prolonged intervention to re-establish and maintain order, and to restore the economy. (The money spent on an operation of that kind would very probably have been more than enough to tide Castro and the Revolution over the crisis of 1959.) This possibility, and all the other variations imaginable, have to be considered as direct consequences of the American decision in 1959 to "let Castro go through the wringer."

Arthur M. Schlesinger, Jr.

KENNEDY AND THE CUBAN PROBLEM

John F. Kennedy's New Frontier program for Latin America found expression in the Alliance for Progress, a liberal solution to social-economic ills that avoided the violence of communism or Castroism. In the following selection, Arthur M. Schlesinger, Jr., Pulitzer prize-winning historian and special assistant to Kennedy, defends Kennedy's Cuban policies and the Alliance. Schlesinger relates the events of the two weeks leading up to the U.S. quarantine of Cuba focusing on the positions taken by the various members of the Executive Committee and the communications between Khrushchev and Kennedy.

KENNEDY'S Latin American interest went back to a tour of South America twenty years earlier. During most of the fifties he had shared the common Washington preference for the problems of Asia until the ferment at the end of the decade—and especially Vice-President Nixon's disastrous trip—renewed his interest in the western hemisphere. Obviously, if the Vice-President were stoned and spat upon in South America, even if one allowed for Nixon's capacity to arouse personal animosity, the position of the United States had declined a good deal since Good Neighbor days. In a speech in Puerto Rico at the end of 1958, a few days before Fidel Castro entered Havana, Kennedy urged that Latin America be given a new priority in United States foreign policy. He warned against the illusion prevalent in North American discussions "that all Latin American agitation is Communist-inspired—that every anti-American voice is the voice of Moscow—and that most citizens of Latin America share our dedication to an anti-Communist crusade to save what we call free enterprise." And

From Arthur M. Schlesinger, Jr., *A Thousand Days: John F. Kennedy in the White House* (Boston, 1965), pp. 191–194, 201–204, 794–813, 820–830. Copyright © 1965 by Arthur M. Schlesinger, Jr. Reprinted by permission of the publisher, Houghton Mifflin Company.

he endorsed a number of specific proposals, including the Inter-American Bank, commodity agreements, loans to encourage land reform and the enlargement of programs of cultural and educational exchange.

Critics of the Eisenhower Latin American policy had been making such points for some time. Perhaps the most influential was Adolf Berle, who, after playing a role in the creation of the Good Neighbor policy, had served Roosevelt as Assistant Secretary of State and as ambassador to Brazil. More than anyone else, Berle provided the link between the Good Neighbor policy and the Alliance for Progress. His experience in Brazil, where he helped in 1945 to set off the train of events leading to the overthrow of the Vargas dictatorship, convinced him that the Good Neighbor policy could not survive as a diplomatic and juridical policy alone. The principle of absolute nonintervention, he felt, did not exhaust the policy; it could only be the first phase in its unfolding. If Good Neighborism did not mean a set of democratic ideas, it would be no more than a policy of sanctifying economic stagnation and political tyranny—a result that would injure the moral position of the United States without furnishing strategic security.

These ideas, in Berle's view, implied not only guarantees against aggression, whether from within the hemisphere or without, but the assurance of basic rights, including the freedoms of expression and political opposition, and the commitment to an economic program which would raise mass living standards. Only these positive elements could create a genuine inter-Americanism based on a community of confidence, not just among governments (which was what nonintervention achieved), but among peoples.

This evolution of the Good Neighbor policy, Berle well understood, required the emergence in Latin America of political leaders and parties committed to democratic objectives. During the forties and fifties, when the State Department was ignoring or harassing Latin American democrats, Berle made it his business to keep in close touch with men like Be-

tancourt and Figueres. In this effort, he worked closely with Luis Muñoz Marín, the remarkable governor of Puerto Rico. Together they developed a network of unofficial relationships with the *partidos populares* of Latin America. Kennedy, whose friendship with Muñoz began with the Puerto Rican trip of 1958, fell heir to these ideas and relationships.

Kennedy's man on Latin America was Richard Goodwin. After graduating from Harvard Law School in 1958, Goodwin came to Washington as law clerk to Justice Frankfurter. He then joined the staff of the House Commerce Committee for its investigation of the television quiz scandals; it was Goodwin who persuaded Charles Van Doren to confess that the quiz shows had been fixed. He went over to Senator Kennedy's office in the fall of 1959 and quickly made himself indispensable. Some, especially in these early years, found his personality, in a favorite Washington word, abrasive. He was certainly driving and often impatient; those whom he overrode called him arrogant. But he was a man of uncommon intelligence, perception and charm. Above all, he had immense facility, both literary and intellectual. He soon proved himself more skilled in writing for Kennedy than anyone but Sorensen; and he also showed himself able to take on any subject, however new and complicated, master its essentials with rapidity and precision and arrive at ideas for action. Kennedy liked his speed, wit, imagination and passion.

Goodwin's friendship with Karl Meyer, who wrote editorials on Latin America for the *Washington Post,* had given him an acquaintance with hemisphere problems and personalities even before he met Kennedy. During the campaign the candidate repeatedly cited Latin America as a signal Republican failure in foreign affairs. When the time approached for a full-dress exposition of Kennedy's own Latin American views, Goodwin was charged with preparing a draft, presumably for delivery at the Alamo. On a campaign bus rolling through Texas in September 1960, he tried to think of a phrase which would express for Kennedy what the phrase Good Neighbor policy had expressed for Roosevelt. As he brooded, his eye happened to catch the title of a Spanish-language magazine which someone had left on the bus in Arizona. The magazine, published by the Alianza Hispano-Americana in Tucson, was called simply *Alianza.* Kennedy agreed that "alliance" should be part of the phrase; but alliance for what? Goodwin telephoned Karl Meyer for suggestions. Meyer then called Ernesto Betancourt, a Cuban who had supported the Castro Revolution but had subsequently broken with Castro and was now working at the Pan American Union. Betancourt proposed two possibilities: *Alianza para el Desarrollo*—Alliance for Development; and *Alianza para el Progreso*—Alliance for Progress. When Meyer reported this, Goodwin laughed and said that Kennedy could not possibly pronounce *Alianza para el Desarrollo.* Moreover, "progress" had the advantage of being essentially the same word in both languages.

*   *   *

But the revolutionary point remained primary. For Kennedy fully understood —this was, indeed, the mainspring of all his thinking about Latin America—that, with all its pretensions to realism, the militant anti-revolutionary line represented the policy most likely to strengthen the communists and lose the hemisphere. He believed that, to maintain contact with a continent seized by the course of revolutionary change, a policy of social idealism was the only true realism for the United States.

Berle, believing on principle that the top State Department man on hemisphere affairs should have the rank of Under Secretary, was unwilling to accept the post of Assistant Secretary for Inter-American Affairs. Instead, Thomas Mann, whom Dillon had transferred to the hemisphere job in August 1960, stayed on in the new administration, and Berle took a somewhat ambiguous appointment as special adviser on Latin American affairs and chairman of a new and now official Latin American Task Force. This was not an altogether satisfactory arrangement. While Berle knew the State Department well, he had always

been something of a loner, and the Foreign Service regarded him with ancient suspicion. Moreover, the professionals mistrusted the new approach to Latin America and were even apprehensive about the phrase "alliance for progress" in the inaugural address. But Mann had played a useful role in helping move hemisphere policy forward in the Eisenhower years; and, though he had an old Latin American hand's skepticism about the grandiose schemes of the New Frontiersmen and, on occasion, even responded a little to the crotchets of Admiral Burke, he was a good bureaucrat and ready enough to go along.

Berle and Mann convened the reconstituted Task Force in February. On February 16, Berle again defined the issue— "to develop policies and programs which would channel the revolution now going on in Latin America in the proper direction and to prevent it from being taken over by the Sino-Soviet bloc." The situation in Latin America, he suggested, resembled that of western Europe in 1947. The Communists had failed then because the Marshall Plan restored western Europe economically while their own opposition to European recovery discredited communism politically. The need now was to confront the Latin American communists with a similar dilemma by offering, so to speak, a moral equivalent of the Marshall Plan, but of course a plan for the development of a continent held down by ignorance and poverty rather than for the reconstruction of a continent rich in managerial and labor skills. The development program, the Task Force agreed, should be on a ten-year basis. It also agreed that new machinery would be necessary; the Inter-American Bank hardly seemed the institution to organize a social revolution. It decided to press for the abolition of the bar against United States assistance to government-owned enterprises. And it concluded by recommending that the President deliver a major address on Latin American policy in the near future.

In the next week, Dick Goodwin began the White House review of Latin American policy in preparation for the presidential speech. He summoned representatives from all agencies having anything to do with Latin America to a meeting in the Fish Room (so called because Roosevelt had placed a stuffed fish on the wall; preserving the tradition, Kennedy now had a large stuffed sailfish of his own catching in the room). After a prolonged canvass of possible projects, Goodwin adjourned the meeting with the request that each agency submit its recommendations within a week. When I got back from Latin America on March 4, I found him sitting in his attic office in the West Wing behind a desk piled high with memoranda from all over the government.

He also consulted with Latin Americans in Washington. On March 8 a document of particular interest came in from the group of Latin American economists who had been foremost in the fight for development—Raúl Prebisch of ECLA, Felipe Herrera of the Inter-American Bank, José A. Mora of the OAS, Jorge Sol of the Inter-American Economic and Social Council, José Antonio Mayobre, the Venezuelan Ambassador, and others. "Latin America," the memorandum began, "is in a state of crisis. Deep-running currents are bringing about great changes in the economic and social structure. These changes cannot and should not be stopped for they stem from needs which, in the present situation of Latin America, permit of no delay." But they must be guided "in order that solutions may be reached which are compatible with the strengthening of fundamental freedoms."

"The responsibility for such changes," the memorandum emphasized, "lies with Latin America," but international cooperation was imperative if they were to come about in a democratic way. Such international interest had to be free from any suspicion of economic imperialism. "The Latin American masses must be convinced that the tremendous task of transferring modern technology to underdeveloped areas . . . has no other aim than the improvement of their lot." Nor could it be supposed that the free play of economic forces alone would bring about the required structural change. "Vigorous state action" was necessary; and it would

not be easy "to overcome the resistance of private groups without disturbances. The policy of cooperation must take this into consideration." The group concluded in somber tones:

We know that Latin America cannot go through the same stages which capitalistic development passed in the course of its historic evolution. We are likewise disturbed at the thought of imitating methods which pursue their economic objectives at the cost of fundamental human freedoms. Latin America still has time to avoid this, but not much time.

* * *

In 1962 the Alliance for Progress was still an uncertainty. As for Castro, increasingly isolated within the hemisphere, he was more bent than ever on the course he had pursued since 1959. "I am a Marxist-Leninist," he said on December 2, 1961, "and I shall be a Marxist-Leninist until the last day of my life"; nor was there any reason to doubt his word. Within Cuba life had settled into drab routine. Economic planners fumbled ineffectually with agricultural and industrial programs. Popular enthusiasm diminished, even if organized opposition did not materially increase. Toward Latin America the regime maintained tenuous relations with half a dozen states and denounced the rest. Toward the United States invective was undefiled, though there were occasional intimations of a desire for something else.

In an accidental encounter after the first Punta del Este conference, Che Guevara told Richard Goodwin that the revolution was irreversible, that Cubans preferred a single-party state headed by Fidel Castro to any alternative and that Cuba's ties with the east were firmly imbedded in a common ideology. At the same time, though, Guevara discussed Cuban economic problems with surprising freedom—bungled planning, shortages in spare parts, in consumer goods and in hard currency reserves—and said that, while any real understanding with the United States would be impossible, what about some sort of *modus vivendi*? He indicated that Cuba might be prepared to pay compensation in trade for expropriated properties and to forswear formal alliance, though not ideological loyalty, to the east. Goodwin saw this—I am sure, quite correctly—as an attempt to persuade Washington to call off the policy of containment before the Latin American governments generalized that policy, as they were soon to do at the second Punta del Este. Castro stated the limits of a *modus vivendi* more exactly on January 23, 1962: "How can the rope and the hanged man understand each other or the chain and the slave? Imperialism is the chain. Understanding is impossible. . . . We are so different that there are no bonds between us. . . . Some day there will be links—when there is a revolution in the United States."

On July 2, 1962, Raúl Castro, the Minister of the Armed Forces, arrived in Moscow. Either before his arrival or very soon thereafter the Soviet and Cuban governments arrived at a startling decision: that Soviet nuclear missiles were to be secretly installed in Cuba in the fall.

The Soviet Union had never before placed nuclear missiles in any other country—neither in the communist nations of Eastern Europe, nor, even in the season of their friendship, in Red China. Why should it now send nuclear missiles to a country thousands of miles away, lying within the zone of vital interest of their main adversary, a land, moreover, headed by a willful leader of, from the Russian viewpoint, somewhat less than total reliability? Castro, with characteristic loquacity, later produced a confusion of explanations. He told a Cuban audience in January 1963 that sending the missiles was a Soviet idea; he repeated this to Claude Julien of *Le Monde* in March 1963; in May he described it to Lisa Howard of the American Broadcasting Company as "simultaneous action on the part of both governments"; then in October he told Herbert Matthews of the *New York Times* that it was a Cuban idea, only to tell Jean Daniel of *L'Express* in November that it was a Soviet idea; in January 1964, when Matthews called him about the Daniel story, Castro claimed again that it was a Cuban idea; and, when Cyrus Sulzberger of the *New York Times* asked him in October 1964, Castro, pleading that the question raised security problems, said cagily, "Both Russia and Cuba participated."

As for the Russians, Khrushchev told the Supreme Soviet in December 1962, "We carried weapons there at the request of the Cuban government . . . including the stationing of a couple of score of Soviet IRBMs [intermediate-range ballistic missiles] in Cuba. These weapons were to be in the hands of Soviet military men. . . . Our aim was only to defend Cuba." The presence of the missiles, Khrushchev continued, was designed to make the imperialists understand that, if they tried to invade Cuba, "the war which they threatened to start stood at their own borders, so that they would realize more realistically the dangers of thermonuclear war." This was all very noble, and the defense of Cuba was certainly a side effect of the Soviet action. But the defense of Cuba did not really require the introduction of long-range nuclear missiles. One may be sure that Khrushchev, like any other national leader, took *that* decision not for Cuban reasons but for Soviet reasons. Pending Khrushchev's reminiscences, one can only speculate as to what these Soviet reasons were.

In a general sense, the decision obviously represented the supreme Soviet probe of American intentions. No doubt a 'total victory' faction in Moscow had long been denouncing the government's 'no-win' policy and arguing that the Soviet Union could safely use the utmost nuclear pressure against the United States because the Americans were too rich or soft or liberal to fight. Now Khrushchev was prepared to give this argument its crucial test. A successful nuclearization of Cuba would make about sixty-four medium-range (around 1000 miles) and intermediate-range (1500–2000 miles) nuclear missiles effective against the United States and thereby come near to doubling Soviet striking capacity against American targets. Since this would still leave the United States with at least a 2 to 1 superiority in nuclear power targeted against the Soviet Union, the shift in the military balance of power would be less crucial than that in the political balance. Every country in the world, watching so audacious an action ninety miles from the United States, would wonder whether it could ever thereafter trust Washington's resolution and protection. More particularly, the change in the nuclear equilibrium would permit Khrushchev, who had been dragging out the Berlin negotiation all year, to reopen that question—perhaps in a personal appearance before the United Nations General Assembly in November—with half the United States lying within range of nuclear missiles poised for delivery across the small stretch of water from Florida. It was a staggering project—staggering in its recklessness, staggering in its misconception of the American response, staggering in its rejection of the ground rules for coexistence among the superpowers which Kennedy had offered in Vienna.

The decision having been made, the next problem was the development of a plan. Moscow evidently saw the operation in two stages—first, the augmentation of Cuban defensive capabilities by bringing in surface-to-air anti-aircraft (SAM) missiles and MIG-21 fighters; then, as soon as the SAMs were in place to protect the bases and deter photographic reconnaissance (a SAM had brought down the U-2 over Russia in 1960), sending in offensive weapons, both ballistic missiles and Ilyushin-28 jet aircraft able to deliver nuclear bombs. The first stage, involving only defensive weapons, required no special concealment. The second stage called for the most careful and complex program of deception. One can only imagine the provisions made in Moscow and Havana through the summer to ship the weapons, to receive them, unload them, assemble them, erect bases for them, install them on launching pads—all with a stealth and speed designed to confront the United States one day in November or December with a fully operational Soviet nuclear arsenal across the water in Cuba.

By late July the Soviet shipments began to arrive. Three weeks later CIA sent an urgent report to the President that "something new and different" was tak-

ing place in Soviet aid operations to Cuba. There were perhaps 5000 Soviet 'specialists' now in Cuba; military construction of some sort was going on; more ships were on their way with more specialists and more electronic and construction equipment. The data suggested that the Soviet Union was refurbishing the Cuban air defense system, presumably by putting up a network of SAM sites.

The intelligence community concluded that Moscow, having resolved after a time of indecision that it had a large stake in Castro's survival, had decided to insure the regime against external attack. It could thereby hope to secure the Soviet bridgehead in the western hemisphere, strengthen Castro's prestige in Latin America and show the world Washington's inability to prevent such things at its very doorstep. This all seemed logical enough. Obviously Moscow had calculated that the United States, with the Bay of Pigs still in the world's recollection, could not convincingly object to Castro's taking defensive precautions against another invasion. No one in the intelligence community (with one exception; for the thought flickered through the mind of John McCone) supposed that the Soviet Union would conceivably go beyond defensive weapons. The introduction of nuclear missiles, for example, would obviously legitimatize an American response, even possibly an invasion of Cuba. Our best Soviet experts in State and CIA considered Khrushchev too wary and Soviet foreign policy too rational to court a risk of this magnitude.

Nonetheless, when a U-2 flight on August 29 showed clear evidence of SAM sites under construction, the President decided to put Moscow on notice. On September 4, the Secretary of State brought over a draft of the warning. The President showed it to the Attorney General, who recommended stiffening it with an explicit statement that we would not tolerate the import of offensive weapons. The draft as revised read that, while we had no evidence of "significant offensive capability either in Cuban hands or under Soviet direction," should it be otherwise, "the gravest issues would arise."

On the same day the Soviet Ambassador in Washington gave the Attorney General an unusual personal message from Khrushchev for the President. The Soviet leader pledged in effect that he would stir up no incidents before the congressional elections in November. Then a week later, in the midst of a long and wearying disquisition on world affairs, Moscow said flatly that the "armaments and military equipment sent to Cuba are designed exclusively for defensive purposes." It added:

There is no need for the Soviet Union to shift its weapons for the repulsion of aggression, for a retaliatory blow, to any other country, for instance Cuba. Our nuclear weapons are so powerful in their explosive force and the Soviet Union has so powerful rockets to carry these nuclear warheads, that there is no need to search for sites for them beyond the boundaries of the Soviet Union.

The statement continued truculently by accusing the United States of "preparing for aggression against Cuba and other peace-loving states," concluding that "if the aggressors unleash war our armed forces must be ready to strike a crushing retaliatory blow at the aggressor." The President responded calmly two days later at his press conference that the new shipments did not constitute a serious threat but that if at any time Cuba were to "become an offensive military base of significant capacity for the Soviet Union, then this country will do whatever must be done to protect its own security and that of its allies." In the meantime, he asked Congress for stand-by authority to call up the reserves.

He had also taken the precaution of doubling the frequency of the U-2 overflights of Cuba. The evidence from flights on September 5, 17, 26 and 29 and October 5 and 7, as well as from other sources, indicated a continuing military build-up large in its proportions but still defensive in its character. The government saw no reason as yet to believe that Khrushchev intended anything beyond this; he had not, so far as we knew, lost his mind. Only John McCone had his personal presentiment that he might be planning the installation of offensive missiles. However, given the prevailing complacency on this point, McCone himself did not take this thought seriously enough to prevent his going off now for a three weeks' honeymoon in Europe. The White House staff worried about this increasingly visible Soviet presence, but it seemed to me much more a political threat to Latin America than a military threat to the United States. I found myself, as I told the President on September 13, relatively a hard-liner and felt that the State Department should tell the Soviet Ambassador in cold and tough fashion that persistence in the arming of Cuba would cause both an increase in our defense budget and a surge of national indignation which would color every other issue between our two countries. But, when I advanced this view at the Bundy staff meeting, I was confronted with the wholly proper question: "OK, but how far would you carry it if they keep on doing what you object to?"

And, across the world, ships were sliding out of Black Sea harbors with nuclear technicians in their cabins and nuclear missiles in their hatches. Khrushchev, having done his best to lull Kennedy by public statements and private messages, now in early September put the second stage of his plan into operation. He could hope that the hurricane season might interfere with the U-2 overflights and that the fall political campaign might inhibit the administration from taking drastic action. Moreover, he had an advantage unknown to us: Soviet engineering had enormously reduced the time required for the erection of nuclear missile sites. As Roberta Wohlstetter, the searching analyst of both Pearl Harbor and the Cuba crisis, later wrote, "The rapidity of the Russians' installation was in effect a logistical surprise comparable to the technological surprise at the time of Pearl Harbor."

In the meantime, Washington had been receiving a flow of tales about nuclear installations through refugee channels. Such reports had been routine for eighteen months. No one could be sure whether the sources in Cuba could tell a surface-to-air from a surface-to-surface missile; moreover, this government recalled that it had been misled by Cuban refugees before. Lacking photographic verification, the intelligence community treated the information with reserve. In the meantime, it recommended on October 4 a U-2 flight over western Cuba. The recommendation was approved on October 10, and from the eleventh to the thirteenth the pilot and plane waited for the weather to break. Sunday the fourteenth dawned beautiful and cloudless.

Senator Kenneth Keating of New York had also been receiving the refugee reports, and he treated them with no reserve at all. At the end of August he began a campaign to force the government into some unspecified form of action. In October he began to talk about offensive missile bases. If he felt the national safety involved, Keating was plainly right to make his case with all the urgency at his command. Some, however, discerned other motives, especially with the approach of the fall election. As Roger Hilsman, Director of Intelligence and Research at the State Department, later wrote, "The charge that Keating was more interested in personal publicity than in his country's welfare may be extreme. But until the Senator comes forward with a better explanation than he has so far supplied, one of two possible conclusions is inescapable: Either Senator Keating was peddling someone's rumors for some purpose of his own, despite the highly dangerous international situation; or, alternatively, he had information the United States Government did not have that could have guided a U-2 to the missile sites before October 14, and at less risk to the pilot."

Now on the fourteenth the U-2 plane returned from its mission. The negatives went swiftly to the processing laboratories, then to the interpretation center, where specialists pored over the blown-up photographs frame by frame. Late Monday afternoon, reading the obscure and intricate markings, they identified a launching pad, a series of buildings for ballistic missiles and even one missile on the ground in San Cristóbal.

About 8:30 that evening the CIA informed Bundy of the incredible discov- ery. Bundy reflected on whether to inform the President immediately, but he knew that Kennedy would demand the photographs and supporting interpretation in order to be sure the report was right and knew also it would take all night to prepare the evidence in proper form. Furthermore, an immediate meeting would collect officials from dinner parties all over town, signal Washington that something was up and end any hope of secrecy. It was better, Bundy thought, to let the President have a night's sleep in preparation for the ordeal ahead.

The President was having breakfast in his dressing gown at eight forty-five on Tuesday morning when Bundy brought the news. Kennedy asked at once about the nature of the evidence. As soon as he was convinced that it was conclusive, he said that the United States must bring the threat to an end: one way or another the missiles would have to be removed. He then directed Bundy to institute low-level photographic flights and to set up a meeting of top officials. Privately he was furious: if Khrushchev could pull this after all his protestations and denials, how could he ever be trusted on anything?

The meeting, beginning at eleven forty-five that morning, went on with intermissions for the rest of the week. The group soon became known as the Executive Committee, presumably of the National Security Council; the press later dubbed it familiarly ExCom, though one never heard that phrase at the time. It carried on its work with the most exacting secrecy: nothing could be worse than to alert the Russians before the United States had decided on its own course. For this reason its members—the President, the Vice-President, Rusk, McNamara, Robert Kennedy, General Taylor, McCone, Dillon, Adlai Stevenson, Bundy, Sorensen, Ball, Gilpatric, Llewellyn Thompson, Alexis Johnson, Edwin Martin, with others brought in on occasion, among them Dean Acheson and Robert Lovett—had to attend their regular meetings, keep as many appointments as possible and preserve the normalities of life. Fortunately the press corps, absorbed in the congressional campaign, was hardly disposed or situated to notice odd comings and goings. And so the President himself went off that night to dinner at Joseph Alsop's as if nothing had happened. After dinner the talk turned to the contingencies of history, the odds for or against any particular event taking place. The President was silent for a time. Then he said, "Of course, if you simply consider mathematical chances, the odds are even on an H-bomb war within ten years." Perhaps he added to himself, "or within ten days."

In the Executive Committee consideration was free, intent and continuous. Discussion ranged widely, as it had to in a situation of such exceptional urgency, novelty and difficulty. When the presence of the President seemed by virtue of the solemnity of his office to have a constraining effect, preliminary meetings were held without him. Every alternative was laid on the table for examination, from living with the missiles to taking them out by surprise attack, from making the issue with Castro to making it with Khrushchev. In effect, the members walked around the problem, inspecting it first from this angle, then from that, viewing it in a variety of perspectives. In the course of the long hours of thinking aloud, hearing new arguments, entertaining new considerations, they almost all found themselves moving from one position to another. "If we had had to act on Wednesday in the first twenty-four hours," the President said later, "I don't think probably we would have chosen as prudently as we finally did." They had, it was estimated, about ten days before the missiles would be on pads ready for firing. The deadline defined the strategy. It meant that the response could not, for example, be confided to the United Nations, where the Soviet delegate would have ample opportunity to stall action until the nuclear weapons were in place and on target. It meant that we could not even risk the delay involved in consulting our allies. It meant that the total responsibility had to fall on the United States and its President.

On the first Tuesday morning the choice for a moment seemed to lie between an air strike or acquiescence—and the President had made clear that acquiescence was impossible. Listening to the discussion, the Attorney General scribbled a wry note: "I now know how Tojo felt when he was planning Pearl Harbor." Then he said aloud that the group needed more alternatives: surely there was some course in between bombing and doing nothing; suppose, for example, we were to bring countervailing pressure by placing nuclear missiles in Berlin? The talk continued, and finally the group dispersed for further reflection.

The next step was military preparation for Caribbean contingencies. A Navy-Marine amphibious exercise in the area, long scheduled for this week, provided a convenient cover for the build-up of an amphibious task force, soon including 40,000 Marines; there were 5000 more in Guantánamo. The Army's 82nd and 101st Airborne Divisions were made ready for immediate deployment; altogether the Army soon gathered more than 100,000 troops in Florida. SAC bombers left Florida airfields to make room for tactical fighter aircraft flown in from bases all over the country. Air defense facilities were stripped from places outside the range of the Cuban missiles and re-installed in the Southeast. As the days went by, 14,000 reservists were recalled to fly transport planes in the eventuality of airborne operations.

In the meantime, the Pentagon undertook a technical analysis of the requirements for a successful strike. The conclusion, as it evolved during the week, was that a "surgical" strike confined to the nuclear missile bases alone would leave the airports and IL-28s untouched; moreover, we could not be sure in advance that we had identified or could destroy all the missile sites. A limited strike therefore might expose the United States to nuclear retaliation. Military prudence called for a much larger strike to eliminate all sources of danger; this would require perhaps 500 sorties. Anything less, the military urged, would destroy our credibility before the world and leave our own nation in intolerable peril. Moreover, this was a heaven-sent opportunity to get rid of the Castro regime forever and re-establish the security of the hemisphere.

It was a strong argument, urged by strong men. But there were arguments on the other side. The Soviet experts pointed out that even a limited strike would kill the Russians manning the missile sites and might well provoke the Soviet Union into drastic and unpredictable response, perhaps nuclear war. The Latin American experts added that a massive strike would kill thousands of innocent Cubans and damage the United States permanently in the hemisphere. The Europeanists said the world would regard a surprise strike as an excessive response. Even if it did not produce Soviet retaliation against the United States, it would invite the Russians to move against Berlin in circumstances where the blame would fall, not on them, but on us. It would thereby give Moscow a chance to shift the venue to a place where the stake was greater than Cuba and our position weaker. In the Caribbean, we had overwhelming superiority in conventional military force; the only recourse for the Soviet Union there would be to threaten the world with nuclear war. But in Berlin, where the Russians had overwhelming conventional superiority, it was the United States which would have to flourish nuclear bombs.

All these considerations encouraged the search for alternatives. When the Executive Committee met on Wednesday, Secretary McNamara advanced an idea which had been briefly mentioned the day before and from which he did not thereafter deviate—the conception of a naval blockade designed to stop the further entry of offensive weapons into Cuba and hopefully to force the removal of the missiles already there. Here was a middle course between inaction and battle, a course which exploited our superiority in local conventional power and would permit subsequent movement either toward war or toward peace.

As the discussion proceeded through Thursday, the supporters of the air strike marshaled their arguments against the blockade. They said that it would not neutralize the weapons already within Cuba, that it could not possibly bring enough pressure on Khrushchev to remove those weapons, that it would permit work to go ahead on the bases and that it would mean another Munich. The act of stopping and searching ships would engage us with Russians instead of Cubans. The obvious retort to our blockade of Cuba would be a Soviet blockade of Berlin. Despite such arguments, however, the majority of the Executive Committee by the end of the day was tending toward a blockade.

That afternoon, in the interests of normality, the President received the Soviet Foreign Minister Andrei Gromyko. It was one of the more extraordinary moments of an extraordinary week. Kennedy knew that there were Soviet nuclear missiles in Cuba. Gromyko unquestionably knew this too, but did not know that Kennedy knew it. His emphasis was rather grimly on Berlin, almost as if to prepare the ground for demands later in the autumn. When the talk turned to Cuba, Gromyko heavily stressed the Cuban fears of an American invasion and said with due solemnity that the Soviet aid had "solely the purpose of contributing to the defense capabilities of Cuba"; "if it were otherwise," the Russian continued, "the Soviet Government would never become involved in rendering such assistance." To dispel any illusion about possible American reactions, the President read the Foreign Minister the key sentences from his statement of September 13. He went no further because he did not wish to indicate his knowledge until he had decided on his course.

In the evening the President met with the Executive Committee. Listening again to the alternatives over which he had been brooding all week, he said crisply, "Whatever you fellows are recommending today you will be sorry about a week from now." He was evidently attracted by the idea of the blockade. It avoided war, preserved flexibility and offered Khrushchev time to reconsider his actions. It could be carried out within the framework of the Organization of American States and the Río Treaty. Since it could be extended to non-military items as occasion required, it could become an instrument of steadily intensifying pressure. It would avoid the shock effect of a surprise attack, which would hurt us politically through the world and might provoke Moscow to an insensate response against Berlin or the United States itself. If it worked, the Russians could retreat with dignity. If it did not work, the Americans retained the option of military action. In short, the blockade, by enabling us to proceed one step at a time, gave us control over the future. Kennedy accordingly directed that preparations be made to put the weapons blockade into effect on Monday morning.

The next day the President, keeping to his schedule, left Washington for a weekend of political barnstorming in Ohio and Illinois. In Springfield, Illinois, after a speech at the State Fairgrounds, he paused to lay flowers on Lincoln's tomb.

Kennedy left behind a curiously restless group of advisers. This became evident when they met at the State Department at eleven on Friday morning. Over Ted Sorensen's protest that a decision had been reached the night before and should not be reopened now, several began to re-argue the inadequacy of the blockade. Someone said: Why not confront the world with a *fait accompli* by taking out the bases in a clean and swift operation? It was a test of wills, another said, and the sooner there was a showdown, the better. Someone else said that it was now or never; we must hit the bases before they became operational. If we took a decision that morning, the planes could strike on Sunday. But, if we committed ourselves to a blockade, it would be hard, if not impossible, to move on thereafter to military action.

Secretary McNamara, however, firmly reaffirmed his opposition to a strike and his support for the blockade. Then Robert Kennedy, speaking with quiet intensity, said that he did not believe that, with all the memory of Pearl Harbor and all the responsibility we would have to bear in the world afterward, the President of the United States could possibly order such an operation. For 175 years we had not been that kind of country. Sunday-morning surprise blows on small nations were not in our tradition. Thousands of Cubans would be killed without warning, and hundreds of Russians too. We were fighting for something more than survival, and a sneak attack would constitute a betrayal of our heritage and our ideals. The blockade, the Attorney General concluded, would demonstrate the seriousness of our determination to get the missiles out of Cuba and at the same time allow Moscow time and room to pull back from its position of peril. It was now proposed that the committee break up into working groups to write up the alternative courses for the President—one to analyze the quarantine policy, the other to analyze the strike. Then everyone dispersed to meet again at four o'clock for a discussion of the competing scenarios.

At the second meeting the balance of opinion clearly swung back to the blockade (though, since a blockade was technically an act of war, it was thought better to refer to it as a quarantine). In retrospect most participants regarded Robert Kennedy's speech as the turning point. The case was strengthened too when the military representatives conceded that a quarantine now would not exclude a strike later. There was brief discussion of a *démarche* to Castro, but it was decided to concentrate on Khrushchev. Then they turned to the problem of the missiles already in Cuba. Someone observed that the United States would have to pay a price to get them out; perhaps we should throw in our now obsolescent and vulnerable Jupiter missile bases in Italy and Turkey, whose removal the Joint Congressional Committee on Atomic Energy as well as the Secretary of Defense had recommended in 1961. After a couple of hours, Adlai Stevenson, who had had to miss the day's meetings because of UN commitments, arrived from New York. He expressed his preference for the quarantine over the strike but wondered whether it might not be better to try the diplomatic route also. We must, he said, start thinking about our negotiating position; for example, a settlement might include the neutralization of Cuba under international guarantees and UN inspection; demilitarization would, of course, include our own base at Guantánamo as well as the Soviet installations. The integrity of Cuba should be guaranteed. He also echoed the suggestion that we might want to consider giving up the Italian and Turkish bases now, since we were planning to do so eventually.

The President, still campaigning, received reports from his brother in Washington. The schedule now called for a speech to the nation on Sunday night. By Saturday morning, however, it was evident that preparations would not be complete in time, so it was decided to hold things for another twenty-four hours. Meanwhile, the President, pleading a cold, canceled the rest of his political trip and returned to Washington. Before leaving Chicago, he called Jacqueline and suggested that she and the children come back from Glen Ora, where they had gone for the weekend.

That afternoon he presided over the Executive Committee and its final debate. McNamara impressively presented the case for the blockade. The military, with some civilian support, argued for the strike. Stevenson spoke with force about the importance of a political program, the President agreeing in principle but disagreeing with his specific proposals. A straw vote indicated eleven for the quarantine, six for the strike. The President observed that everyone should hope his plan was not adopted; there just was no clearcut answer. When someone proposed that each participant write down his recommendation, Kennedy said he did not want people, if things went wrong, claiming that their plans would have worked. Then he issued orders to get everything ready for the quarantine. On Sunday morning a final conference with the military leaders satisfied him that the strike would be a mistake. His course was now firmly set.

I knew nothing about any of this until late Friday, October 19, when Adlai Stevenson phoned me, saying casually that he was in Washington and wondered when we could get together. He was staying at the house of his friend Dr. Paul Magnuson across the street from my own house in Georgetown, and we agreed to ride down to the State Department together the next day. When we met after breakfast on Saturday morning, he beckoned me into the Magnuson house. "I don't want to talk in front of the chauffeur," he said; and then in a moment, "Do you know what the secret discussions this week have been about?" I said I knew of no discussions; the President was out campaigning; I had presumed that everything was fine. Adlai, observing gravely that there was trouble and he had the President's permission to tell me about it, described the seesaw during the week between the diplomatic and military solutions. The quarantine, he now felt, was sure to win. He would have to make a speech early in the week at the Security Council, and he wanted me to help on it. He outlined the argument and, with due discretion, I set to work.

The secret had been superbly kept. But later in the day, when the President returned from the campaign and Rusk canceled a speech that night, a sense of premonitory excitement began to engulf Washington. Already those whose business it was to sniff things out were on the track. In the British Embassy, where a delegation of intelligence officers had come to Washington for a long-scheduled conference with the CIA, suspicions had been aroused early in the week when the meetings drew a diminishing American representation or were called off altogether. By process of elimination the 007s decided on Friday that it must be Cuba. The *New York Times,* noting the troop movements and other unusual activities, also deduced Cuba by the weekend and even speculated about nuclear missiles. James Reston wrote the story and checked it with the White House. The President himself called Orville Dryfoos, the publisher of the *Times,* to say that publication might confront him with a Moscow ultimatum before he had the chance to put his own plans into effect; once again, the *Times* killed a story about Cuba. By Saturday night the town was alive with speculation and anticipation. A good deal of the government found itself late that evening at a dance given by the James Rowes. Here the gap between the witting and the unwitting could almost be detected by facial expressions—on the one hand, anxiety tinged with self-satisfaction; on the other, irritation and frustration. Henry Brandon, the Washington correspondent of the London *Sunday Times*, who had just returned from a trip to Cuba, began to wonder when a succession of top officials asked him elaborately offhand questions about the mood in Havana.

On Sunday Stevenson, contemplating the problems of gathering UN backing for the quarantine, wrote down his thoughts about our UN strategy. He saw no hope of mustering enough votes in the UN to authorize action against Cuba in advance; but the OAS offered an opportunity for multilateral support, and OAS approval could provide some protection in law and a great deal in public opinion. As for the UN, he said, we must seize the initiative, bringing our case to the Security Council at the same time we imposed the quarantine. In order to avert resolutions against the quarantine, he continued, we should be ready to propose a political path out of the military crisis. His negotiating program, following his remarks to the Executive Committee, centered on the removal of Soviet military equipment and personnel—i.e., missiles, installations and the several thousand Russian specialists—under UN observation and the introduction of UN influence into Cuba in the hope of ending communist domination of the Cuban government. He would throw a non-invasion guarantee and Guantánamo into the bargain to evidence our restraint and good faith. Exercising the prerogative freely employed that week by nearly all his colleagues, he now wrote that Turkey and Italy should not be included; this would only divert attention from the Cuban threat to the general issue of foreign bases. That problem might later be considered apart from Cuba in the context of general disarmament.

The President, however, rightly regarded any political program as premature. He wanted to concentrate on a single issue—the enormity of the introduction of the missiles and the absolute necessity for their removal. Stevenson's negotiating program was accordingly re-jected. Stevenson, when I saw him that week-end, took this realistically; he felt he had done his job as the custodian of our UN interests in making the recommendation, and the decision was the President's. However, some of his colleagues on the Executive Committee felt strongly that the thought of negotiations at this point would be taken as an admission of the moral weakness of our case and the military weakness of our posture. They worried considerably over the week-end (and some of them vocally thereafter) whether, denied his political program, Stevenson would make the American argument with sufficient force in the UN debate.

I spent all day Sunday till well after midnight working at the State Department with Harlan Cleveland, Joseph Sisco and Thomas Wilson on the UN speech. At ten o'clock on Monday morning the President called me in to instruct me to go to New York and assist Stevenson on the UN presentation. He was in a calm and reflective mood. It was strange, he said, how no one in the intelligence community had anticipated the Soviet attempt to transform Cuba into a nuclear base; everyone had assumed that the Russians would not be so stupid as to offer us this pretext for intervention. I asked why he thought Khrushchev had done such an amazing thing. He said that, first, it might draw Russia and China closer together, or at least strengthen the Soviet position in the communist world, by showing that Moscow was capable of bold action in support of a communist revolution; second, that it would radically redefine the setting in which the Berlin problem could be reopened after the election; third, that it would deal the United States a tremendous political blow. When I remarked that the Russians must have supposed we would not respond, Kennedy said, "They thought they had us either way. If we did nothing, we would be dead. If we reacted, they hoped to put us in an exposed position, whether with regard to Berlin or Turkey or the UN."

I met with him again at eleven to go over the draft of the UN speech with Rusk, Robert Kennedy and others. The

President suggested a few omissions, including a passage threatening an American strike if the Soviet build-up in Cuba continued; he preferred to leave that to Moscow's imagination. The Attorney General drew me aside to say, "We're counting on you to watch things in New York. . . . We will have to make a deal at the end, but we must stand absolutely firm now. Concessions must come at the end of negotiation, not at the beginning." Then, clutching the speech, I caught the first plane to New York.

In Washington everything awaited the President's television broadcast that night to the nation. Sorensen had been laboring over the draft since Friday. Kennedy himself was never more composed. At four o'clock he had an appointment with Prime Minister Milton Obote of Uganda. Wholly at ease, he talked for forty-five minutes about the problems of Africa and Uganda as if he had nothing on his mind and all the time in the world. Angier Biddle Duke of the State Department remarked to Obote on their way back to Blair House that a crisis of some sort was imminent; the Ugandan was incredulous and, when he heard Kennedy's speech that evening, forever impressed.

At five o'clock Kennedy saw the congressional leaders, many of whom had flown in from their home states in Air Force planes. He showed them the U-2 photographs and told them what he proposed to do. Senator Russell of Georgia disagreed; the quarantine, he said, would be too slow and too risky—the only solution was invasion. To the President's surprise, Fulbright, who had opposed invasion so eloquently eighteen months before, now supported Russell. The President listened courteously but was in no way shaken in his decision. (Kennedy told me later, "The trouble is that, when you get a group of senators together, they are always dominated by the man who takes the boldest and strongest line. That is what happened the other day. After Russell spoke, no one wanted to take issue with him. When you can talk to them individually, they are reasonable.")

Then at seven o'clock the speech: his expression grave, his voice firm and calm,

the evidence set forth without emotion, the conclusion unequivocal—"The purpose of these bases can be none other than to provide a nuclear strike capability against the Western Hemisphere." He recited the Soviet assurances, now revealed as "deliberate deception," and called the Soviet action "a deliberately provocative and unjustified change in the status quo which cannot be accepted by this country, if our courage and our commitments are ever to be trusted again by either friend or foe." Our "unswerving objective," he continued, "was to end this nuclear threat to the Americans. He then laid out what he called with emphasis his *initial* steps: a quarantine on all offensive military equipment under shipment to Cuba; an intensified surveillance of Cuba itself; a declaration that any missile launched from Cuba would be regarded as an attack by the Soviet Union on the United States, requiring full retaliatory response upon the Soviet Union; an immediate convening of the Organization of American States to consider the threat to hemisphere security; an emergency meeting of the UN Security Council to consider the threat to world peace; and an appeal to Chairman Khrushchev "to abandon this course of world domination, and to join in an historic effort to end the perilous arms race and to transform the history of man."

He concluded with quiet solemnity. "My fellow citizens: let no one doubt that this is a difficult and dangerous effort. . . . No one can foresee precisely what course it will take or what costs or casualties will be incurred. . . . But the greatest danger of all would be to do nothing. . . . Our goal is not the victory of might, but the vindication of right—not peace at the expense of freedom, but both peace *and* freedom, here in this hemisphere, and, we hope, around the world. God willing, that goal will be achieved."

* * *

Within the Kremlin, so far as one could tell, there was confusion. The Russians had obviously anticipated neither the quick discovery of the bases nor the quick imposition of the quarantine. Their diplomats across the world were displaying all the symptoms of improvisation, as if they had been told nothing of the placement of the missiles and had received no instructions what to say about them. Ambassador Anatoly Dobrynin himself gave every indication of ignorance and confusion. As late as Wednesday a message to Robert Kennedy from Mikoyan repeated that Cuba was receiving no weapons capable of reaching the United States. Georgi Bolshakov, who transmitted the message and who had seemed to us all an honest fellow, assured the Attorney General that he believed this himself.

In New York on Wednesday Stevenson was continuing the battle for the American resolution in the United Nations. John J. McCloy, whom the President had summoned from a business trip to Germany to give the UN presentation a bipartisan flavor, was adding his weight to our councils. Then U Thant made an unexpected intervention, proposing that the Soviet Union suspend its arms shipments and the United States its quarantine to allow an interlude for negotiations. Khrushchev accepted this thought at once and with evident pleasure; but, from our viewpoint, it equated aggression and response, said nothing about the missiles already in Cuba, permitted work to go forward on the sites and contained no provisions for verification. Still, while New York and Washington agreed in rejecting U Thant's proposal, the manner of the rejection caused debate. Some in Washington appeared to fear any response which would 'entrap' us in a negotiating process; it seemed to us in New York that they must be bent to clear the road for an air strike and an invasion. Stevenson and McCloy strongly recommended a response to U Thant which would keep the diplomatic option alive.

On Wednesday night, as we were pondering these matters at the U.S. Mission in New York, I received a telephone call from Averell Harriman. Speaking with unusual urgency, he said that Khrushchev was desperately signaling a desire to cooperate in moving toward a peaceful solution. Harriman set forth the evidence: Khrushchev's suggestion of a summit meeting in his reply to Bertrand Russell; his well-publicized call on the American singer Jerome Hines the night before after a Moscow concert; his amiable if menacing talk with an American businessman, William Knox of Westinghouse International; the indications that afternoon that the nearest Soviet ships were slowing down and changing course. This was not the behavior of a man who wanted war, Harriman said; it was the behavior of a man who was begging our help to get off the hook. Khrushchev had sent up similar signals after the U-2 affair in 1960, Harriman continued, and Eisenhower had made the mistake of ignoring him; we must not repeat that error now. "If we do nothing but get tougher and tougher, we will force him into countermeasures. The first incident on the high seas will engage Soviet prestige and infinitely reduce the chance of a peaceful solution." The key to it all, he went on, lay in Khrushchev's two remarks during the recent visit of Robert Frost and Stewart Udall to the Soviet Union—his observation to Frost that the democracies were too liberal to fight and his observation to Udall that the Soviet Union must be treated as an equal. "We must give him an out," Harriman said again. "If we do this shrewdly, we can downgrade the tough group in the Soviet Union which persuaded him to do this. But if we deny him an out, then we will escalate this business into a nuclear war."

These words from the most experienced of all American diplomats seemed utterly convincing to me. I asked him whether he had made these points at the State Department. He said, "They never ask my advice about anything outside the Far East. I haven't been in on this at all." Accordingly I sent Harriman's views along to the President. Kennedy called him the next morning, and I imagine that Harriman's counsel may have strengthened his own inclination to go further along the diplomatic road. At any rate, his reply to U Thant on Thursday, while stressing that the "threat was created by the secret introduction of offensive weapons into Cuba, and the answer lies in the removal of such weapons," authorized Stevenson to continue discussions on whether satisfactory arrangements could be assured to this end. This was a second vital decision.

In Washington they had meanwhile been seeking to provide for every contingency the quarantine might create. By involving us directly with the Russians, it contained a great variety of potential risks; and the Executive Committee undertook the most intensive consideration of all possible gradations and configurations: where, when and how to stop ships, how much force to use, when to board, whether to disable the propeller and tow the ship to port. Soon they ascertained that Soviet submarines were following the ships; as quickly as possible, we put a destroyer on the tail of every submarine. It was all an amazing naval deployment, conducted with skill and efficiency. Among the destroyers to take part, apparently in the natural line of duty, was the *Joseph P. Kennedy, Jr.*

As they plotted the courses and studied the charts, Thursday seemed to confirm the encouraging signs of Wednesday and to justify Ormsby Gore's suggestion of Tuesday night that the line of interception be drawn closer to Cuba. Half the Soviet ships, the Executive Committee noted with a flood of relief, had put about and were heading home. Others were evidently waiting for further orders. Only one had entered the quarantine zone—a tanker, obviously not carrying nuclear weapons. In Washington some felt that we must react to this challenge with full military vigor; but the President decided to give Khrushchev more time and said that the tanker, once it had identified itself and thereby established the quarantine, should be permitted to proceed without boarding and search—a third vital decision.

There were other portents, and to them our intelligence community turned like Roman haruspices to the entrails of a sacrificial victim. For the first time all that long week Soviet diplomatic behavior across the world was beginning to conform to a pattern; this indicated that Moscow had at last sent out instructions. For one thing—and very odd in view of our own and the British apprehension about Soviet reprisals in Berlin—the Russians appeared to be engaged in a studied effort to dissociate Berlin from Cuba. Gromyko, who spoke at Humboldt University in East Berlin on Tuesday, instead of using the occasion for implied threats, did not even mention Cuba. By Friday V. A. Zorin, the Soviet ambassador to the United Nations, was even assuring other UN diplomats that his government would not fall into the American "trap" of retaliatory action in Berlin.

But the essence of the emerging pattern seemed to be concern for a peaceful settlement. This was what the Soviet ambassadors in London and Bonn were saying to the British and West German governments. Nor was Moscow confining its efforts to orthodox channels. In London on Wednesday, for example, Captain Ivanov of the Soviet Embassy asked a demimondain doctor named Stephen Ward to use his influence to persuade the British government to invite Khrushchev and Kennedy to a summit meeting. Ward thereupon approached Lord Arran, a peer who wrote a column in the *Evening News*, and even sent a letter to Harold Wilson, whom he did not know. Thwarted in these efforts to solve the world's problems, he soon returned to the more relaxed company of Christine Keeler.

But despite these gestures the situation was still loaded with danger. Work continued on the sites; unless this was stopped, the missiles would soon be on their launching pads. Nor had the Soviet Union yet admitted the presence of nuclear missiles in Cuba at all. On Thursday evening at the UN Stevenson returned to the debate in the Security Council. He crisply dismissed the communist argument that the United States had created the threat to the peace: "This is the first time that I have ever heard it said that the crime is not the burglary, but the discovery of the burglar." As for those who thought the quarantine too extreme a remedy: "Were we to do nothing until the knife was sharpened? Were we to stand idly by until it was at our throats? . . . The course we have chosen seems to me perfectly graduated to meet the character of the threat."

Zorin made a cocky but evasive reply.

Now Stevenson took the floor again. Ironically regretting that he lacked his opponent's "talent for obfuscation, for distortion, for confusing language and for double-talk," saying sternly "those weapons must be taken out of Cuba," he turned on the Russian with magnificent scorn:

Do you, Ambassador Zorin, deny that the USSR has placed and is placing medium and intermediate-range missiles and sites in Cuba? Yes or no? Don't wait for the translation. Yes or no?

Zorin muttered something about not being in an American courtroom. Stevenson, cold and controlled:

You are in the courtroom of world opinion. You have denied they exist, and I want to know if I understood you correctly. I am prepared to wait for my answer until hell freezes over. And I am also prepared to present the evidence in this room—now!

It was a moment of tremendous excitement. At Stevenson's order, aerial photographs were wheeled on easels into the council chamber, showing the transformation of San Cristóbal from a peaceful country spot into a grim nuclear installation. Other pictures added further evidence. Zorin wanly denied the authenticity of the display. Stevenson wondered savagely why the Soviet Union did not test its denial by permitting a United Nations team to visit the sites.

Then, in a moment, Stevenson concluded: "We know the facts and so do you, sir, and we are ready to talk about them. Our job here is not to score debating points. Our job, Mr. Zorin, is to save the peace. And if you are ready to try, we are."

The Stevenson speech dealt a final blow to the Soviet case before world opinion.

But on Friday work still continued on the sites. In Florida the American army prepared for invasion. In Washington the pressure to attack mounted as each passing moment brought the installations closer to operation. And in Moscow there must have been deep anxiety and bitter debate.

Khrushchev had now evidently abandoned the effort to bring in more nuclear weapons. But some of the men around him—perhaps the Soviet military—were apparently determined to make the missiles already there operational as speedily as possible. Indeed, this group may have gone along with the pacific gestures of Wednesday and Thursday precisely to gain time to complete the sites. In any case, once the missiles were on launching pads, Moscow might be able to drive a better bargain.

Khrushchev himself, however, seems to have reached a different position. He knew by now that his essential gamble had failed. Whatever he had once supposed, the Americans were ready to fight. His own options were narrowing before his eyes. If he were to strike at Berlin, he would only expose the Soviet Union to nuclear attack. If he did not compose matters quickly in the Caribbean, then the great army, massing so visibly in Florida, would descend on Cuba; "on the morning of [Saturday] October 27," as he told the Supreme Soviet in December, "we received information that the invasion would be carried out in the next two or three days." If an invasion began, Khrushchev either would have to use the rockets he liked to boast about so jovially or else desert the only communist state in the Americas and condemn himself as a *fainéant* before the international communist movement. It was now beyond the realm of tactical maneuver: all roads led to the abyss. The Soviet Chairman and the American President were the two men in the world with ultimate responsibility for nuclear war. Like Kennedy, Khrushchev had peered into the abyss before. "Immediate action," as he later told the Supreme Soviet, "was needed to prevent an invasion of Cuba and to preserve peace."

At one-thirty on Friday John Scali, the State Department correspondent for the American Broadcasting Company, received a call from Aleksander Fomin, a counselor at the Soviet Embassy, insisting on an immediate meeting. Scali, who had lunched occasionally with Fomin in the past, joined him at once at the Occidental Restaurant. The usually phlegmatic Russian, now haggard and alarmed, said, "War seems about to break out. Something must be done to save the situation." Scali replied that they should have thought of that before they put the missiles in Cuba. The Russian sat in silence for a moment. Then he said, "There might be a way out. What would you think of a proposition whereby we would promise to remove our missiles under United Nations inspection, where Mr. Khrushchev would promise never to introduce such offensive weapons into Cuba again? Would the President of the United States be willing to promise publicly not to invade Cuba?" When Scali said he did not know, Fomin begged him to find out immediately from his State Department friends. Then, reaching for a pencil, he wrote down his home telephone number: "If I'm not at the Embassy, call me here. This is of vital importance."

Scali carried the proposal to Roger Hilsman at State, and Hilsman carried it to Rusk. After discussion with the Executive Committee, Rusk asked Scali to tell the Russian that we saw "real possibilities" for a negotiation but they must understand that time was short—no more than forty-eight hours. At seven-thirty Friday evening Scali passed this word along. They met this time in the coffee shop of the Statler Hilton. Fomin, once he had satisfied himself about the authenticity of Scali's message and after a brief attempt to introduce the idea of UN inspection of Florida as well as Cuba, rose and, in his haste to get the word back, tossed down a five-dollar bill for a thirty-cent check and speeded off without waiting for the change.

Two hours later a long letter from Khrushchev to the President began to come in by cable. The Soviet leader started by insisting that the weapons shipments were complete and that their purpose was defensive. Then he declared his profound longing for peace; let us, he said with evident emotion, not permit this situation to get out of hand. The enforcement of the quarantine would only drive the Soviet Union to take necessary measures of its own. But if the United States would give assurances that it would not invade Cuba nor permit others to do so and if it would recall its fleet from the quarantine, this would immediately change everything. Then the necessity for a Soviet presence in Cuba would disappear. The crisis, Khrushchev said, was like a rope with a knot in the middle: the more each side pulled, the more the knot would tighten, until finally it could be severed only by a sword. But if each side slackened the rope, the knot could be untied.

The letter was not, as subsequently described, hysterical. Though it pulsated with a passion to avoid nuclear war and gave the impression of having been written in deep emotion, why not? In general, it displayed an entirely rational understanding of the implications of the crisis. Together with the Scali proposal, it promised light at the end of the cave. And in New York on Friday we heard that Zorin had advanced the same proposal to U Thant, and that the Cubans at the UN were beginning to hint to unaligned delegates that the bases might be dismantled and removed if the United States would guarantee the territorial integrity of Cuba. The President probably had his first good night's sleep for ten days; certainly the rest of us did.

But when the Executive Committee assembled on Saturday morning, prospects suddenly darkened. The Moscow radio began to broadcast a new Khrushchev letter containing, to everyone's consternation, an entirely different proposition from the one transmitted through Scali and embodied in Khrushchev's letter of the night before. The Soviet Union now said it would remove its missiles from Cuba and offer a nonaggression pledge to Turkey if the United States would remove its missiles from Turkey and offer a nonaggression pledge to Cuba. The notion of trading the Cuban and Turkish bases had been much discussed in England; Walter Lippmann and others had urged it in the United States. But Kennedy regarded the idea as unacceptable, and the swap was promptly rejected. This proposal was perplexing enough; but, far more alarming, word soon came that a U-2 was missing over Cuba, presumably shot down by the Russians (piloted, indeed, by the brave South Carolinian, Major Rudolph Anderson, Jr., who had first photographed the installations on October 14). American planes had thus far flown over the missile sites without interference. The Soviet action now, some felt, could only mean one thing: that the confrontation was entering its military phase. The bases were becoming operational, and the Russians were evidently determined to use force to maintain them. We had no choice, it was argued, but a military response; and our tactical analysis had already shown that strikes at the bases would be little use without strikes at the airfields, and strikes at the airfields of little use without further supporting action, so, once the process began, it could hardly stop short of invasion.

The President declined to be stampeded. Obviously, if they shot down U-2s, we would have to react—but not necessarily at once. Again he insisted that the Russians be given time to consider what they were doing before action and counteraction became irrevocable. There remained the Khrushchev letters, and the Executive Committee turned to them again with bafflement and something close to despair. It was noted that Defense Minister Rodion Malinovsky had mentioned Cuba and Turkey together as early as Tuesday, and that *Red Star,* the army paper, had coupled them again on Friday. Could the military have taken over in Moscow? Rusk called in Scali and asked him to find out anything he could from his Soviet contact. Scali, fearful that he had been used to deceive his own country, upbraided Fomin, accusing him of a double cross. The Russian said miserably that there must have been a cable delay, that the Embassy was waiting word from Khrushchev at any moment. Scali brought this report immediately to the President and the Executive Committee at the White House (where Pierre Salinger nearly had heart failure when, in the midst of the rigorous security precautions of the week, he suddenly saw the ABC reporter sitting at the door of the President's inner office).

In the meantime a new crisis: another U-2 on a routine air-sampling mission from Alaska to the North Pole had gone off course and was over the Soviet Union; it had already attracted the attention of Soviet fighters and was radioing Alaska for help. Would the Russians view this as a final reconnaissance in preparation for nuclear attack? What if they decided to strike first? Roger Hilsman brought the frightening news to the President. There was a moment of absolute grimness. Then Kennedy, with a brief laugh, said, "There is always some so-and-so who doesn't get the word." (The plane returned safely; but perhaps Khrushchev did interpret the flight exactly as Hilsman feared; perhaps this too, along with the invasion force massing in Florida and an unauthorized statement on Friday by the State Department press officer threatening "further action" if work continued on the bases, reinforced his determination to bring the crisis to an end.)

Later that afternoon the Executive Committee met again. Robert Kennedy now came up with a thought of breathtaking simplicity and ingenuity: why not ignore the second Khrushchev message and reply to the first? forget Saturday and concentrate on Friday? This suggestion may, indeed, have been more relevant than anyone could have known. For . . . the so-called second letter, from internal evidence, appears to have been initiated as the immediate follow-on of Khrushchev's reply to U Thant; it began with a reference to Kennedy's reply to U Thant on Thursday and took no note of events on Friday. Moreover, its institutional tone suggested that it was written in the Foreign Office. Might it not have been drafted in Moscow on Thursday and Friday with an eye to Saturday morning release in New York? Then the so-called first letter, which reflected the movement of events well beyond the U Thant proposal and which was clearly written by Khrushchev himself, may well have been composed late Friday night (Moscow time) and transmitted immediately to Kennedy while the "second" letter was deep in the bureaucratic pipelines. Knowing heads of state and foreign office bureaucracies, one could take anything as possible.

At any rate, on October 27 Kennedy

now wrote Khrushchev, "I have read your letter of October 26th with great care and welcomed the statement of your desire to seek a prompt solution." As soon as work stopped on the missile bases and the offensive weapons were rendered inoperable under UN supervision, Kennedy continued, he would be ready to negotiate a settlement along the lines Khrushchev had proposed. Then, in a sentence profoundly expressive of his desire to retrieve something out of crisis, he added: "If your letter signifies that you are prepared to discuss a detente affecting NATO and the Warsaw Pact, we are quite prepared to consider with our allies any useful proposals."

And so the message shot inscrutably into the night. Robert Kennedy carried a copy that evening to the Soviet Ambassador, saying grimly that, unless we received assurances in twenty-four hours, the United States would take military action by Tuesday. No one knew which Khrushchev letter superseded the other; no one knew whether Khrushchev was even still in power. "We all agreed in the end," Robert Kennedy said afterward, "that if the Russians were ready to go to nuclear war over Cuba, they were ready to go to nuclear war, and that was that. So we might as well have the showdown then as six months later." Saturday night was almost the blackest of all. Unless Khrushchev came through in a few hours, the meeting of the Executive Committee on Sunday might well face the most terrible decisions.

Sunday, October 28, was a shining autumn day. At nine in the morning Khrushchev's answer began to come in. By the fifth sentence it was clear that he had thrown in his hand. Work would stop on the sites; the arms "which you described as offensive" would be crated and returned to the Soviet Union; negotiations would start at the UN. Then, no doubt to placate Castro, Khrushchev asked the United States to discontinue flights over Cuba. (As for the errant U-2 which had strayed over Russia the day before, he warned that "an intruding American plane could be easily taken for a nuclear bomber, which might push us to a fateful step.") Looking ahead, he said, "We should like to continue the exchange of views on the prohibition of atomic and thermonuclear weapons, general disarmament, and other problems relating to the relaxation of international tension."

It was all over, and barely in time. If word had not come that Sunday, if work had continued on the bases, the United States would have had no real choice but to take action against Cuba the next week. No one could discern what lay darkly beyond an air strike or invasion, what measures and countermeasures, actions and reactions, might have driven the hapless world to the ghastly consummation. The President saw more penetratingly into the mists and terrors of the future than anyone else. A few weeks later he said, "If we had invaded Cuba . . . I am sure the Soviets would have acted. They would have to, just as we would have to. I think there are certain compulsions on any major power." The compulsions opened up the appalling world of inexorability. The trick was to cut the chain in time. When Kennedy received Khrushchev's reply that golden October morning, he showed profound relief. Later he said, "This is the night to go to the theater, like Abraham Lincoln."

Daniel Tretiak

CUBA AND THE SOVIET UNION:

THE GROWING ACCOMMODATION, 1964–1965

Daniel Tretiak wrote the following selection while associated with the Rand Corporation, although the article does not reflect that organization's views. The manner by which Cuba was incorporated into the Soviet bloc was not without tension and discord; both Cuba and the Soviet Union had to make political and ideological adjustments.

WHILE many of the present communist party-states became members of the communist system as a result of external coercion after World War II, some have joined that system because of ideological affinity, coupled with the expectation that national interests would be adequately met by this move. For some of these, entry has brought net gains; for others, membership has not automatically led to the satisfaction of material expectations. The experiences of the latter group have modified their relations with either the leader of the system, the USSR, or its rival, China. Thus far none of the states in the system has completely severed ties with Moscow.

The loose bipolarity in international affairs over the past twenty years has helped those nation-states that are not aligned politically with either the Soviet Union or the United States to maintain a relatively neutral position between the two major power blocs. Moreover, the national interests of individual member-states within each of the blocs have generally operated to erode the control of the bloc leader. This trend has prevailed in spite of frequent setbacks to national aspirations and temporary restorations of bloc-leader authority.

Cuba's role in the postwar international environment has been exceptional. Interaction with the United States, its political mentor for over fifty years, has virtually ceased; Cuba has pledged its allegiance—reluctantly, in some respects, at first—to the USSR, and over a period of several years has become increasingly integrated into the communist system.

Cuba's role as a Soviet-sponsored communist state has not been achieved without tension. But there has been a gradual expansion and consolidation of mutually beneficial relations between the two countries. Because the Cuban Revolution represented a sharp break with Cuba's past pattern of internal policies and external relations, its leaders struggled for several years before they could attain the stability and institutionalization necessary in order to alter the relations entered into by previous regimes.

CUBA'S CHINESE AND SOVIET OPTIONS

The severance of Cuban-U.S. relations in 1961 left it to the USSR to meet Cuba's excessively ambitious economic and political demands. Difficulties developed at an early date for Cuban-USSR diplomacy when Castro persisted in his plan to "make the Andes the Sierra Maestras of Latin America," for this implicitly contradicted Moscow's policy of seeking a détente with the United States. Especially after the missile crisis of 1962,

From Daniel Tretiak, "Cuba and the Soviet Union: the Growing Accommodation, 1964–1965," *Orbis*, XI (Summer, 1967), pp. 439–458. Reprinted by permission of *Orbis*, a quarterly journal of world affairs published by the Foreign Policy Research Institute of the University of Pennsylvania and courtesy of the author.

Latin American communist parties were on the whole unresponsive to Cuba's call for revolution. Their attitude aggravated Castro's doubts of Soviet support for Cuba's national interests.

Throughout the period 1961–1964, when Cuba was attempting to play a dynamic international role in the Caribbean and in Latin America, the Cuban government had to deal with serious internal divisions over political and economic policy. Political disputes that had disturbed relations between the Partido Socialista Popular (PSP, the Cuban Communist Party) and the virtually unorganized 26th of July Movement from 1956 to 1958 continued to prevent a genuine fusion between the two groups. In spite of this, a single political organization, the Organización Revolucionaria Integrada (ORI), was proclaimed in 1961. The lack of genuine cohesion slowed down membership recruitment, formulation of a party constitution and establishment of a party hierarchy. It also resulted, beginning in 1962, in the expulsion from the ORI of certain PSP leaders.

At this time Cuba's economic goals, like those of other underdeveloped countries, were based on the belief that Cuban political independence could best be safeguarded by increasing economic independence through industrialization. They reflected orthodox Marxist doctrine, as well as the emotional reaction of many Cubans against excessive emphasis on sugar production. But these goals were impractical, as the Cubans have been forced to admit, because Cuba lacked the political and economic experience necessary to attain them in a brief period of time. In 1960 Havana had asked the leading communist states to pledge support for its industrialization program. The Soviet Union was unwilling to provide economic aid without assurances as to its proper use. As for the Chinese, they simply lacked the economic resources to meet their commitment, even though they realized that the Chinese emphasis on armed struggle in Latin America was appealing to some, if not all, Cuban elites. Moscow's response, particularly, caused resentment in Cuba.

Not fully satisfied with either Moscow or Peking, the Cuban leadership was unwilling to support either government in the momentous dispute that began to unfold publicly between them as Cuba entered the communist orbit. On some issues the Cubans seemed to side with the Chinese, thus further inhibiting the development of smooth relations between Havana and Moscow. But, on the whole, in 1963 and 1964 they remained neutral in their response to the Sino-Soviet dispute.

Economically, the Cubans were heavily dependent on the USSR. Soviet trade (much of it really aid) accounted for about 45 per cent of Cuba's total trade turnover from 1961 through 1964; China's share amounted to 10 per cent in the same period, making China Cuba's second best trading partner. Given the fragile basis of Cuba's economy, the Cubans had good reason to avoid antagonizing the Chinese, especially after the Soviets turned out to be less reliable supporters of the Revolution than they had hoped. But interest in Chinese friendship should not be interpreted to mean that Cuba, at any time during 1961–1964, was growing closer to China than to the Soviet Union. During this period its dealings with the Soviet bloc were consistently more intensive than its intercourse with the Chinese and their adherents. Only on certain key issues such as the nuclear test ban treaty and the spread of armed revolution did Havana tend to side with Peking against Moscow.

The discussion that follows shows how various areas of Soviet-Cuban conflict began to be resolved by the end of 1964. Cuban resentments subsided appreciably after the 1962 missile crisis and with the easing of Cuba's economic dilemma; the Soviets, particularly after Khrushchev's ouster, took steps to increase Cuba's organizational prestige with the Latin American communist parties, and the Cubans, especially after January 1965, responded in kind to Soviet overtures. Even at times of relatively high tension between the two governments, the benefits accruing to the Cubans from adherence to the communist sphere provided an effective basis for Soviet-Cuban accommodation.

PARTIAL RESOLUTION OF SOVIET-CUBAN DIFFICULTIES

During 1965, the main irritants that had marked Soviet-Cuban relations since 1961, such as the debate over the correct means for communist parties to take power and the direction of Cuba's economic development, were at least partially removed. The Cubans had consistently maintained that if communists or other leftists were to replace noncommunist governments in Latin America, it would be necessary to resort to armed struggle. The Soviets disapproved this policy, but even more to the point, Latin American communist parties were unwilling to follow Cuban advice because they felt it was inappropriate in various countries.

By the end of 1963, earlier Soviet attempts to settle their policy differences with the Cubans having proved fruitless, new initiatives were required. Premier Castro visited Moscow in January 1964 at Khrushchev's request. He accepted Soviet guarantees of price-supports for sugar as a partial *quid pro quo* for postponing industrialization. Although not entirely satisfied with this arrangement, he was willing to acquiesce in it, meanwhile denying publicly that industrialization was being sacrificed. Nevertheless, Cuba continued through the autumn of 1964 to refrain from noticeably supporting the USSR in the Sino-Soviet dispute, refusing, for example, to sign the nuclear test ban treaty.

Meanwhile, Soviet Latin American policy—the "peaceful way"—failed conspicuously to bring communists to power in Brazil and Chile in 1964. Such setbacks implied that Chinese and Cuban criticism might not have been baseless; they may well have played some part in Khrushchev's downfall. The fact that for a month after his ouster the Cubans were as silent about it as the Chinese, no doubt reflected their underlying resentment at Khrushchev's demands concerning Cuban foreign and domestic policy. They may have felt that their abstention from

public criticism of the new Soviet leadership deserved to be rewarded by some concessions, especially in the area of foreign policy. In late November, when the Chinese began to attack the new leadership in the Kremlin, the Cubans sought to strengthen their relations with the Soviet Union.

Amelioration of Ideological Tensions. Havana's hopes were rewarded in part. A Conference of the Communist Parties of Latin America was held in Havana at the end of 1964. The meeting was secret, the final communiqué was unsigned, but all Latin American parties apparently were represented. Soviet observers were present, but the Chinese were neither present nor invited. Where a party was split into pro-Chinese and pro-Soviet groups (e.g., Brazil, Peru, Chile), only the pro-Soviet faction was represented.

On the issue of support for the Cuban Revolution and armed struggle, the communiqué tended to mollify Cuban sensitivities:

With regard to supporting the struggle of the other people in Latin America against imperialism, the Conference formulated the following recommendations: [it called on the communist parties] to support actively those who are actually suffering repression such as Venezuelan, Colombian, Guatemalan, Honduran, Paraguayan, and Haitian combatants.

The communiqué also called on the communist parties to associate themselves publicly with Cuba by demanding that their governments officially recognize the Castro regime and oppose the U.S.-sponsored blockade of Cuba. It advocated "a publicity campaign about all the successes of the Cuban Revolution—economic, social, and cultural." Although the document did not specifically support armed struggle as the only correct road to power, it paid particular attention to the Venezuelan, Colombian and Guatemalan paramilitary campaigns.

According to the communiqué, the participants at the meeting took neither side in the Sino-Soviet dispute, although the views of the Chinese on several points at issue in the communist movement were tacitly criticized. First, the communiqué called for "multilateral meetings (*encuentros*) and a conference (*reunión*) or conferences of all Marxist-Leninist parties, which may be necessary." Second, it declared that "all factional activity [within the various parties] ought to be categorically repudiated." Third, it recommended "immediate cessation of public polemics" in the Sino-Soviet dispute.

These three positions of the conference represented agreement with Soviet policy at the expense of the Chinese. Cuba was willing to concur with the Soviet stand because of the communiqué's praise and support of the Cuban Revolution and of the armed struggles proceeding on the Latin American continent. The Cubans felt that enough was offered to them, both in the communiqué itself and in the fact that the meeting was held in Havana, to justify measures to ease their political relations with the Soviet Union. The communist parties attending the conference did not promise to follow the Cubans on all issues. Nevertheless, the meeting gave a new standing and legitimacy within the communist movement to the Cuban leadership and the Cuban party organization.

Castro used the communiqué of the Latin American communist meeting as the basis of his remarks in a speech of March 13, 1965. After recalling Soviet-Cuban discord during the missile crisis, he turned to the Sino-Soviet dispute, stating that it only benefited "our enemies" and Cubans had "a perfect right to abolish, to banish that discord and those Byzantine battles from [their] country. . . ." According to Castro, Cubans "do not understand the language of division." His charges were directed against China, which had maintained a polemical tone in its communications with the Soviets.

Castro further implied that the Chinese had accused the Cubans of not supporting the Viet Cong strongly enough against the Americans. In response, he sternly proclaimed: ". . . let no one imagine he can lecture to us on revolutionary behavior." It was the duty of "the socialist camp" to accept whatever risks might be necessary in Viet Nam.

Cuba's attendance at the Moscow meeting of communist parties in March 1965 was another important manifestation of the new attitude of accommodation toward the Soviet Union. The Cuban delegation was led by Raúl Castro. Cuban press attention to the conference was consistently high, while the Chinese boycotted it and later criticized its participants.

The Economic Debate Partially Settled. The Soviets agreed to provide some degree of support for Castro's revolutionary goals in return for which the Cuban leader redefined earlier economic goals to match Soviet support levels and exhorted Cubans to proceed apace with the development first of sugar production, and second of cattle raising. Castro's reshuffling of the Instituto Nacional para Reforma Agraria (INRA) and his speeches on Cuba's economy made it clear that agriculture would be the basis for that economy, at least for several years to come.

In early February 1965, Castro removed Carlos Rafael Rodríguez from the presidency of INRA, assuming that position himself. This change and the designation of 1965 as the "Año de la Agricultura" (The Year of Agriculture) set the stage for several pronouncements by the Cuban Premier on future agricultural development. He de-emphasized plans for Cuba's industrialization, noting that in the past three years the "development of our economy and the role agriculture plays in this development have expanded. Agriculture has been changed so that today it is the basis for the economic development of our country."

He also described how the entire party-state apparatus would have to be used in support of agriculture if the country's economic goals were to be met:

Agriculture requires not only the effort of the Party but . . . of all other organizations, because neither agriculture nor . . . [the party] alone can effect these tasks. They can be realized by putting all the forces of the Party to work with the full support of other administrative organs, on which agriculture greatly depends.

The Ministry of Industry would have to subordinate itself to the goals of the

INRA: "The Ministry of Industry can play a very important role . . . and we will depend on [it] to a great extent for fulfilling [our agricultural plans]."

While Castro was advocating continued emphasis on the Cuban sugar industry and giving some support to the Soviet leaders in their dispute with the Chinese, Che Guevara was taking positions abroad that clearly ran counter to Castro's efforts to improve Soviet-Cuban relations.

THE GUEVARA DISAPPEARANCE

The formation of a Cuban party apparatus was a slow and tortuous process culminating in the establishment of an official Cuban Communist Party early in October 1965. This organization superseded the ORI and the Partido Único de la Revolución Socialista (PURS); its leadership, like that of its predecessors, was increasingly drawn not from the old PSP, the pre-revolutionary communist party, but from the ranks of Castro's 26th of July Movement. The near-totality of the PSP eclipse was manifested sharply at this time. Of 104 new members on the party's Central Committee less than 20 per cent were from the old PSP. Former PSP members Blas Roca and Carlos Rafael Rodríguez are among the six members of the Secretariat, but all eight members of the Politburo come from the old July 26th Movement.

The naming of the new party executive coincided with the announced departure from the upper echelons of Ernesto ("Che") Guevara, an Argentinian who had joined Castro's movement in 1956, was long Castro's alter ego, and enjoyed second place in the Cuban ruling elite after 1959. Guevara's disappearance from the Cuban political scene—announced on October 3, 1965—far outshadowed the removal or eclipse of any previous revolutionary figures. It was, in fact, a contribution to the resolution of the controversial issues that kept Cuba and the Soviet Union apart. Although Castro's earlier attitudes toward these questions had delayed Cuba's integration into the communist community, he had come to recognize more clearly than Guevara the need to strengthen ties with the USSR, despite costs to Cuban internal and international goals. It was therefore necessary to dissociate Guevara's opposite views from Cuba's official policy.

As this realignment in policy was being put into effect—between November 1964 and March 1965—Guevara was out of Cuba. Nevertheless, on various occasions he indicated his dissatisfaction with the decline of interest in rapid industrialization. He also noted that Soviet aid left something to be desired, and called for a reaffirmation of the Cuban commitment to revolution overseas. Guevara's statements in other countries were his last published remarks on outstanding issues involving Cuba and the communist part of the world.

From mid-December to mid-March, Guevara was on an African tour similar to the 1964 trip of Chinese Premier Chou En-lai. He visited Algeria, Mali, Congo (Brazzaville), Dahomey and Ghana, then went to China for approximately a week. In Africa again, he stopped briefly in Tanzania and the UAR, revisited Algiers, and returned to the UAR. After a stop in Prague, he arrived back in Cuba on March 15, and soon thereafter disappeared from public view.

Hoy's March 21 issue carried a picture of Guevara reporting to personnel in the Ministry of Industry about his trip; his remarks have not been published. By the time he returned from his travels, the Cuban leadership's decision to speed up the accommodation with the Soviets not only required the Revolution to sacrifice more of its neutrality in the Sino-Soviet dispute, but also made it necessary to remove Guevara from power so as to silence his influential but now impolitic views. His African trip revealed the limited international appeal of his policies precisely when a little foreign support might have strengthened his position at home.

In Africa Guevara had hoped to gain support for his charge that "U.S. imperialism" was "the first common problem" facing both Cuba and Africa. Moreover, he maintained that broader economic ties could be used to strengthen Cuban-African relations, which presently were slight. He noted that "Cuba has sugar, cattle, and nickel; Ghana, cacao; Algeria, oil. If we were all to unite, [we could obtain] the most sophisticated derivatives of each product, and large industrial combines could be formed that would serve a substantial group of countries." He also restated his views stressing industrialization over the intensification of agricultural production—in direct conflict with his country's new policy of developing the sugar industry. He stressed industrial and mining goals for Cuba, and virtually excluded mention of the then-current drive to re-emphasize sugar:

Cuba proposed to develop to the maximum its capacity for utilizing its raw materials in order to take advantage of its [present] installed capacity and to develop its consumer-goods industries to the maximum, and also to make a geological survey and a most thorough investigation of natural resources.

Guevara reiterated his belief in the primacy of armed struggle among the ways to power. On one occasion he said that "with very few exceptions, the taking of power in Latin America will be through armed struggle," although conceding that other strategies might be successful in Latin America and Africa.

The Africans refused to accept his main tenets. Of the seven countries he visited—Algeria, Ghana, Mali, Dahomey, Congo (Brazzaville), the UAR and Tanzania—only the governments of Ghana and Mali signed joint communiqués. These revealed that Guevara's failure to influence the Africans was nearly total. For example, neither Ghana nor Mali specifically denounced "U.S. imperialism"; neither endorsed Guevara's call for wider Cuban-African trade—or, in Ghana's case, even some minimal form of economic cooperation. While all parties pledged support to rebels in the Portuguese colonies, no sanction of Guevara's guerrilla warfare theories appeared in either communiqué.

When nearing the end of his trip, Guevara remarked in Dar-es-Salaam, Tanzania's capital, that "before embarking on this African trip, I feared that Africa was unaware of the danger posed by U.S. imperialism, which has bound up its

politics with so-called aid programs. Nevertheless, after meeting with African statesmen, I can say that these African countries are clear on this question." He was correct; they were clear enough on this question and other questions to refuse to embroil themselves in Cuba's problems. They also seemed unwilling to enter into meaningful political and economic cooperation with Cuba. Communiqués were the only face-saving gestures two of the more radical African countries—Ghana and Mali—could provide Guevara. He returned home, his views rejected by the Africans who did not want to endanger their relations with the USSR and China by becoming allies of Cuba.

Guevara's dealings with the Africans were more delicate than were his remarks about the Soviets and certain issues relevant to internal Cuban politics. In Algiers, he implicitly criticized the Soviet Union for price discrimination in foreign trade with the underdeveloped nations. Speaking as a special guest at the Second Economic Seminar of Afro-Asian Solidarity, Guevara said:

The development of the countries which are now embarking upon the road of liberation must be borne by the Socialist countries. . . . We believe that this responsibility for aid to the dependent countries must be met in [a fraternal] spirit, and that there should be no talk of mutually beneficial trade based on the prices which the law of value and the international relations of unequal exchange, a product of the law of value, impose upon the underdeveloped countries.

How can "mutual benefit" mean the sale at world market prices of the raw materials which cost the backward countries sweat and boundless suffering, and the purchase of the machines produced in today's large automated factories at world market prices? If we establish this type of relation between the two groups of nations, then we must agree that the socialist countries are, to a certain extent, accomplices in the imperialist exploitation. . . . Socialist countries have a moral duty to remove all tacit complicity with the exploiting countries of the West.

Guevara was also critical of the communist states' unwillingness to supply arms to "liberation movements" free of charge. He remarked:

If it is absurd to think of a director of an enterprise in a Socialist country at war hesitating to send tanks to the front which cannot guarantee payment, no less absurd is it to think of a man who sees the possibility of payment from a nation which is fighting for its freedom or which needs these weapons to defend its freedom. Weapons cannot be considered salable goods in our world. They must be given without charge and in the necessary quantities to the extent possible, to the nations requesting them, to fire at the common enemy.

As if to minimize the sharpness of his criticism, he added:

This is the spirit in which the USSR and the CPR gave us their military aid. We are socialists; we constitute a guarantee for the use of these weapons. However, we are not the only ones. U.S. imperialism's ominous attack upon Vietnam or the Congo must be answered by supplying these sister nations with all the instruments necessary to their defense and by giving them our complete and unconditional solidarity.

Guevara was clearly directing his criticisms against the USSR: it was the Soviets at that time, far more than the Chinese, who were insisting that Cuban trade be on a more businesslike basis; it was the Soviets, especially in relation to Viet Nam and the Congo, who were doing less militarily to aid "national liberation movements" than they were capable of doing. The Chinese had provided both advisers and funds for the rebels in the Congo; only in response to the Belgian-American airlift did Moscow indirectly release arms to aid the rebellion.

After his Algiers visit, Guevara traveled back to Egypt. In an interview reported in the Arabic-language journal, *Al Tali-'ah*, he not only resurrected early PSP/July 26th Movement differences within the Cuban Communist Party, but also attacked the Yugoslavs for various revisionist economic schemes (a favorite device of the Chinese for criticism of the Soviets). He claimed that during the 1957–1958 period the PSP

committed grave mistakes. Perhaps this basic error was due to its failure to strike

a deep understanding of the magnitude of the spread of the revolutionary movement and the possibilities which lay in struggle; thus it always lagged behind the movement which rose under the leadership of Fidel Castro.

He also reviewed a 1962 Cuban purge directed against pro-Soviet PSP leaders.

Guevara associated himself by implication with the Chinese against the Soviets in his criticism of Yugoslav economic innovations, expressing concern that "where production law dominates [the economy], it surrenders the economy to capitalism. That is to say that in Yugoslavia, there is danger of walking toward capitalism, and it is imminent that this economic principle [capitalism] shall reflect on its political position." While his criticisms of the Yugoslavs may have been directed only at Tito's regime, they had anti-Soviet undertones. In Algiers, Guevara had unmistakably questioned Moscow's economic motives; in Cairo, he broadened the scope of his public disagreement with the Soviets.

Like the Africans, the Chinese were apparently unimpressed by Guevara's policy statements; they paid very little heed to his presence in Africa. *Pravda* and *Izvestiia* did not report it at all. Moreover, upon visiting China in February 1965, Guevara met with a curious reception: he talked to high party functionaries, yet did not meet Chairman Mao. No substantial account of his visit appeared in the Chinese press. At home, *Hoy* simply mentioned Guevara's arrival in Canton, but carried no further news of his whereabouts until he reached Tanzania. According to some reports, the Chinese were desirous that Cuba stay away from the Moscow Conference to be held the next month. Guevara could not commit Cuba to this deviation, not only because he was far from Havana, but also because he knew that the Cubans were going to attend the meeting, regardless of his own position. Indeed, the Chinese may have known that the Cubans would go to the meeting and they may simply have used this opportunity to express to Guevara their disenchantment with Castro and his followers.

FURTHER INDICATORS OF SOVIET-CUBAN ACCOMMODATION

Cuban Behavior at "Front" Meetings. Cuba's increasingly open support of the Soviets rather than the Chinese was manifested during July 1965 at the meetings of the World Peace Council (WPC) in Helsinki, Finland; the Anti-Atomic and Hydrogen Bomb meeting in Nagasaki, Japan; the Executive Committee of the World Federation of Trade Unions (WFTU) in Prague; and in its reaction to the aborting of the Ninth World Youth Festival, scheduled for Algiers at the end of that month.

The World Congress on Peace, National Independence and Disarmament was held in Helsinki July 10–15. Previously, Cuban delegates to such meetings had been low-level personages; this time Juan Marinello, one-time president of the PSP, headed the delegation. Unlike Cuban press treatment of similar "front" meetings in earlier years, reportage of this meeting was thorough.

On the other hand, Cuba made its position known by its absence from the Eleventh World Conference Against Atomic and Hydrogen Bombs, held in Nagasaki from July 1–8. At the previous year's meeting, the Soviet delegation, in response to an open Sino-Soviet difference of opinion, had walked out. The Cubans had stayed, playing a minor role in the proceedings. In 1965, fully aware that the meeting would be Chinese-dominated, they followed the Soviet example and sent no representatives to Nagasaki.

The Ninth World Youth and Student Festival was to have been held in Algiers at the end of July. But when the Ben Bella government was overthrown by a military coup, the Soviet Union, the East European party-states (Albania excepted) and Cuba reacted harshly to the new Boumedienne government. In contrast, the Chinese supported the new regime and hoped that the Youth Festival, as well as the earlier scheduled Afro-Asian meeting, would still be held.

The Cuban leadership—Fidel Castro especially—was vociferous in its denunciation of the anti-Ben Bella coup. Disagreeing with the Chinese, Cuba joined the Soviets in urging that the festival not be held in Algiers in 1965. In order to preserve a semblance of Sino-Cuban amity, the Chinese criticism of those who advocated postponement omitted an attack on the Cubans.

The Executive Committee of the World Federation of Trade Unions (WFTU) met in Prague July 13–17. Although Cuban participation in the WFTU had previously been sporadic, Lázaro Peña, head of the Confederación de Trabajadores Cubanos (Revolucionaria) [CTC(R)], had held a prominent position in the world organization since the days of Batista. At the July Executive Committee meeting, the Cubans not only were represented by Peña, but also voiced approval of Soviet policy. They made no criticism of Moscow's policy toward Viet Nam, while the Chinese claimed that the Soviets "talked a lot about unity and anti-imperialism, but [that] their actions did not suit their words." In opposition to the Chinese view that the Executive Committee meeting would lead to greater disunity within the WFTU, the Cuban assertion, as expressed by Peña, was that the sessions had "strengthened the classical and anti-imperialist stand of the organization."

Cuba and CMEA. Despite the large number of bilateral treaties, protocols, conventions and contracts between Cuba and individual communist states, relations between Cuba and the Council for Mutual Economic Assistance (CMEA, or COMECON) have been slow to develop. Because of general doubts among its members about the wisdom of dispensing foreign aid to the Cubans, CMEA has been reluctant to formalize relations with Havana. On their side, the Cubans, while willing to take as much aid as possible from the party-states, have been hesitant to join such organizations as CMEA lest broad-scale economic plans inimical to their national interests be imposed on them. The Cubans have not wanted to subject their economic goals to overall bloc planning, fearing that their hopes for industrialization might be sacrificed. Cuban press reports of attendance and observation at CMEA meetings have been very rare until recently.

During 1965, the change in Cuba's relations with CMEA was not as perceptible as that in connection with the "front" organizations. Nevertheless, a few interesting developments occurred. In January the Cubans attended the Nineteenth Executive Committee Meeting of CMEA— the first time a Cuban observer is reported to have attended such a meeting. A functionary of the Cuban Foreign Trade Ministry, Cristóbal Victorero, subsequently attended another CMEA meeting in mid-March of 1965.

These might have been signs that the Cuban leadership was considering an intensification of relations with CMEA. However, of twelve CMEA meetings held during June and July 1965, a Cuban observer attended only one, that for Ferrous Metallurgy. Even China and Yugoslavia participated in more of the sessions. Moreover, the Cuban press did not report any of the twelve meetings considered.

In October 1965, a Cuban scientific delegation headed by the vice-president of the Cuban Academy of Sciences visited the Dubna nuclear research institute outside Moscow. Later the Cubans, but not the Chinese, North Vietnamese, North Koreans or Albanians, were invited to participate with seven other party-states in a space-research project under Soviet auspices. Vice-Prime Minister and Minister of the Armed Forces Raúl Castro attended the joint maneuvers of four Warsaw Pact nations in October, the first time a leading Cuban military figure was reported present at such a gathering. Quite clearly, Cuban relations with functional organizations of the communist system are expanding.

Cuban Attention to Other Communist Parties. From 1962 through most of 1964, the Partido Unido de la Revolución Socialista (PURS) was a more feeble organization than its successor, the Cuban Communist Party, and its external associations were limited. In order to maintain their neutrality in the Sino-Soviet dispute, the Cubans had kept relations with all other communist parties to a minimum, and there were few reports of developments in other parties in the Cuban press.

However, as Cuba's relations with the Soviets and their followers improved, attention to the activities and statements of the pro-Soviet party increased markedly. During the period July–December 1964, of 18 stories appearing in *Hoy* about various communist parties (or far-left political groups), 14 (78 per cent) dealt with pro-Soviet organizations and 4 (22 per cent) with pro-Chinese groups or individuals (e.g., the Brazilian Francisco Julião and the Guatemalan guerrilla, Marco Antonio Yong Sosa). None of the items had to do with pro-Chinese communist parties per se, or splinter groups of pro-Soviet parties. During the shorter five-month period, January–May 1965, of 39 stories in *Hoy* dealing with communist parties, 37 (95 per cent) were about pro-Soviet parties and only two (5 per cent) about pro-Chinese organizations. These figures suggest a change in Cuban policy away from neutrality, or occasionally implied support of the Chinese, toward a consolidation with the Soviets.

Chinese Disenchantment with the Cubans. During the post-1959 period the Chinese were convinced that the Cuban Revolution would herald the spread of other revolutions in Latin America. The Cubans shared this hope, frequently encouraging Latin Americans to carry on protracted armed struggles against existing governments. The Soviets were less enthusiastic about such activity, although some pro-Soviet Latin American communist parties (Venezuelan, Guatemalan) associated themselves with guerrilla fighters. But the Cuban Revolution was not duplicated elsewhere, and Cuba became politically, if not spiritually, isolated from Latin America; in 1962 the Organization of American States excluded her from membership. The Chinese continued to maintain a keen interest in Cuban political and economic life, hoping to turn Sino-Cuban ideological affinity into support for Chinese positions against those of the Soviets.

Then, concurrent with the sharp increase in Soviet-Cuban interaction, there was a striking decline in Chinese approval of the Castro regime and its external policies. By the end of 1964, Sino-Cuban relations had already reached their apogee; in early 1965 a waning of mutual attraction began, and this continued during 1966. The 1965 shift in positions is revealed by comparing Chinese and Soviet reports of Castro's speeches, Cuba's response to major international crises, and economic developments in Cuba.

In 1963 and 1964 the Chinese regularly reprinted speeches by Fidel Castro, Raúl Castro, and Che Guevara; they reprinted no speeches of these three Cuban leaders from January to May 1965. In contrast, the Soviets, who had reprinted Cuban speeches less regularly than had the Chinese in selected periods in 1964, increased their coverage of Castro speeches not only in *Pravda* and *Izvestiia*, but also in external publications and those of pro-Soviet communist parties.

In 1965—as compared to 1964—the Chinese also showed their disapproval of Cuban foreign policy responses by scarcely mentioning those responses in the Chinese papers. For example, after the August 5, 1964 Tonkin Bay incident in Viet Nam, *Jenmin Jihpao* reprinted Cuban statements about the American involvement on August 7 and 10 as well as Castro's discussion of the bombing. Cuban comments about the United States setting up an airlift in the Congo in December 1964 were also well reported. In contrast, after the first U.S. air-strike against North Viet Nam (February 7, 1965) and the U.S. dispatch of troops to the Dominican Republic, Chinese reports of Cuban responses were virtually non-existent, even though strong protests were registered against these U.S. actions within Cuba.

Finally, while in previous years the Chinese had consistently reported Cuban economic developments, only one article about the Cuban economy appeared in *JMJP* (on February 8) during the January–June 1965 period. The Chinese perceived by early 1965 that the Cubans were no longer neutral in the Sino-Soviet dispute.

Although the Chinese themselves have refrained from publicly criticizing Cuban behavior, some of their ideological allies have been less restrained. During 1965, the Albanians, the pro-Chinese Belgian communists, and certain Latin Americans in accord with Chinese ideological views grew critical of Cuba's more pro-Soviet posture.

Cuban Disinterest in China. The increasing disinterest in Cuban affairs shown by the Chinese press was matched to a certain extent by a similar inattention to Chinese affairs in Cuban papers. While the number of articles in *Hoy* in 1965 about miscellaneous developments involving China did not decrease significantly in comparison with 1964, attention given to the activities of the Chinese leadership fell off markedly. Cuban coverage of Chou En-lai's visit to several African countries in January 1964 was far more complete than it was with respect to Chou's 1965 travels. Mao Tse-tung's statement on the U.S.-Belgian airlift from the Congo was reported in Hoy at the end of 1964, but there were no reprints of Mao's statements on key international problems in 1965.

CONCLUSION

Cuba's developing affinity with the Soviet Union led to a near-break in Sino-Cuban relations in early 1966. A bitter Sino-Cuban debate was carried on within the framework of foreign trade, although in fact the Chinese were criticizing Cuban behavior in the Sino-Soviet dispute and alleged Cuban compromise on the issue of aid to armed revolutions. By attacking Castro, the Chinese were joining with advocates of guerrilla warfare, especially in Latin America, as well as with certain Cuban elites (probably in the Cuban armed forces) who were critical of Castro's accommodation with the Soviet Union and the Guevara ouster.

As if to re-establish Cuba's revolutionary credentials, Havana played host in January 1966 to the Tri-Continental Conference of communist delegations meeting to promote the coordination of "national liberation wars." Cuba subsequently became the site of the Secretariat of the Organization of Solidarity of the Peoples of Asia, Africa and Latin America (OSPAAAL) established by the conference. Nevertheless, the Chinese and those who shared their views remained dissatisfied with Cuban behavior. Consequently, since mid-1966, the Cubans have begun to strengthen their ties with noncommunist revolutionary organizations in various Latin American countries, at the expense of good relations with orthodox communist parties. Cuban criticism of those unwilling to pursue violence against incumbent regimes in Latin America is reminiscent of the early 1960's. While the Soviets have not been overly enthusiastic in support of this Cuban attitude, they have preserved a position of importance in Cuba, continuing, for example, to lend extensive assistance in the development of the sugar industry.

Apart from having to tolerate policy disagreements with its new junior partner, the USSR's monetary costs for economic support of the Cuban Revolution have remained quite high. Because of this, however, the Soviets could successfully exert pressure on Cuba to modify its economic development goals. Once the Cubans agreed to Moscow's insistence that agriculture, especially sugar-growing, should be emphasized and industrialization decelerated in line with Cuban capabilities, they embarked on an ambitious program to grow large amounts of sugar cane. In 1965 the sugar crop exceeded six million tons. The Cubans expect that production will increase to ten million tons by 1970, although the 1966 total of 4,452,718 tons represented a 1.6 million ton drop from the 1965 level. They also hope that Soviet aid will be invested primarily in mechanization of harvesting, improvement of mill operating capacity, and training of technicians capable of handling machinery. If goals for production are consistently met over the coming five years, Cuba may find herself with an efficient, mechanized sugar industry, profits from which could underwrite the coveted industrialization.

Although the Cubans have in effect pushed the problem of industrialization under the rug, one issue remains to be faced. Cuba is an urban, not a rural country. The Havana government knows full well that while investment in sugar production may represent a wise allotment of Soviet resources, the Cuban urbanite is simply unwilling to "volunteer" for work in the *Zafra* (sugar cane harvest). The combination of forced labor and minimal mechanization has been successful to date, but the government would prefer to provide jobs in the city for urban dwellers, not force them to work in the countryside because there are too few city jobs available. It is possible that the Cubans agreed to emphasize sugar production on condition that some funds would be diverted to industrialization and technician training for factories in the cities. Even so, the cost to Cuba from even temporary concentration on stepped-up agriculture may be great. The huge exodus of Cuban refugees to the United States is partly the result of sacrificing the urbanization goal, for there simply were not enough jobs to employ urban workers. Rather than risk an uprising from the urban areas, Castro was able to convince the United States, in effect, to alleviate potential stress on his regime by accepting the influx of refugees.

If, by 1970, sugar production has been significantly increased and a serious, well-prepared foundation for industrialization laid, Cuba will have overcome its initial economic failures and will be a relatively stable member of the communist system. It may also have the strength to re-establish its neutral, yet potentially dynamic, position within that system. Meantime its experience is an example of how the system—and the Soviet Union in particular—has the capability to attract other states to it despite not inconsequential differences, and to provide for most, if not all, a new system-member's needs when that member is willing to accommodate, even subordinate, itself to system goals.

SUGGESTIONS FOR ADDITIONAL READING

The following selections are general introductions to the history of Cuba from the Spanish conquest to the present: Willis Fletcher Johnson, *The History of Cuba* (5 vols., New York, 1920), an older but still reliable account; Charles E. Chapman, *History of the Cuban Republic* (New York, 1927), which concentrates primarily on the years 1903–1926; and Hudson Strode, *The Pageant of Cuba* (New York, 1936), which traces Cuban history into the early 1930s, when Batista rose to power. For the student who reads Spanish, there is the *Historia de la nación cubana* (10 vols., Havana, 1952), the contribution of Cuban scholars.

United States policy in Cuba has attracted a number of scholars. The latest summary of this topic is Lester D. Langley, *The Cuban Policy of the United States: A Brief History** (New York, 1968), which concentrates on important episodes in Cuban-American relations (the filibustering expeditions of the 1850s, the Ten Years' War, the Spanish-American War, *etc.*) and interprets American policy in the twentieth century as a continuation of nineteenth century attitudes. Related studies are David Healy, *The United States in Cuba, 1898–1902* (Madison, 1963); Robert F. Smith, *The United States and Cuba: Business and Diplomacy, 1917–1960** (New York, 1961), which is especially strong on the relationship between capital and diplomacy in U.S.-Cuban affairs; and Russell H. Fitzgibbon, *Cuba and the United States, 1900–1935* (New York, 1964; orig. pub., 1935), which is still a very useful work. Dana G. Munro, *Intervention and Dollar Diplomacy in the Caribbean, 1900–1921* (Princeton, 1964); Bryce Wood, *The Making of the Good Neighbor Policy** (New York, 1961); and Donald Dozer, *Are We Good Neighbors? Three Decades of Inter-American Relations, 1900–1960* (Gainesville, 1959), discuss Cuba in the context of the Latin American policy of the United States.

An adequate history of United States relations with Batista and Castro is yet to be written. Wyatt McGaffey and Clifford Barnett have provided a good introduction in *Twentieth Century Cuba: The Background of the Castro Revolution* (Garden City, 1965). Edmund Chester's *A Sergeant Named Batista* (New York, 1954) is adulatory and unreliable. Specialists in the field have offered their views in John N. Plank, ed., *Cuba and the United States: Long-Range Perspectives* (Washington, 1967), which discusses the past but speculates on the future. Phillip Bonsal, Smith's successor in Havana, offers his observations on the Cuban-American rift in "Cuba, Castro, and the United States," *Foreign Affairs,* XLV (January, 1967), pp. 260–276. Kennedy advisers Arthur M. Schlesinger, Jr., and Theodore Sorensen relate the crucial episodes—the Bay of Pigs and the Missile Crisis—in detailed fashion in *A Thousand Days: John F. Kennedy in the White House* (Boston, 1965), and *Kennedy* (New York, 1965). Haynes Johnson, *et al., The Bay of Pigs: The Leaders' Story of Brigade 2506* (New York, 1964) reveals the plight of the invaders who failed to destroy Castro's government in April, 1961. Elie Abel and Henry Pachter have described the terrifying days of October, 1962, in *The Missile Crisis* (Philadelphia, 1966), and *Collision Course** (New York, 1963). Abel writes from the viewpoint of a news commentator, and Pachter, from the analytical framework of a political scientist. A handy collection of documents is contained in David Larson, ed., *The Cuban Crisis of 1962: Selected Documents and Chronology** (Boston, 1963). The legal question in the Cuban quarantine of 1962 is debated in Charles G. Fenwick, "Quarantine Against

* available in paperback

Cuba: Legal or Illegal," *American Journal of International Law,* LVII (July, 1963), pp. 588–599, which defends the American government's position; and Quincy Wright, "The Cuban Quarantine," *ibid.,* pp. 546–565, which adopts a critical view.

The "real" Castro is yet to be captured in print. Analyses completed in the late 1950's or early 1960's, such as Herbert Matthews, *The Cuban Story* (New York, 1961), an account by the *New York Times* reporter who visited Castro in the Sierra Maestra in 1957; or Theodore Draper, *Castro's Revolution: Myths and Realities** (New York, 1962), which emphasizes the role of Cuba's middle classes in Batista's overthrow, are still reliable but must be used with care. Castro's image as a heroic leader is a central theme in Ward Morton, *Castro as a Charismatic Hero* (Lawrence, Kansas, 1965), and Teresa Casuso, *Cuba and Castro* (New York, 1961), written by an alienated Castroite.

There is a historiographical gap between those works composed during the years when Castro was enjoying his role as a harassed revolutionary-in-power and accounts written after 1962, when Castro the Marxist-Leninist led Cuba into the Soviet orbit. Some, such as Maurice Zeitlin and Robert Scheer, *Cuba: Tragedy in Our Hemisphere** (New York, 1963),

never made the transition from writing anti-American, pro-Castro tracts to more detailed, objective analyses. Fortunately, others have. For instance, Andrés Suárez, a former Castro official, portrays the Cuban dictator as a skillful politician in *Cuba: Castroism and Communism, 1959–1960* (Cambridge, Massachusetts, 1967). Suárez has not allowed himself to become the spokesman for the anti-Castro right.

Gradually, scholarship is moving toward greater objectivity. In this category there are James O'Connor, "On Cuban Political Economy," *Political Science Quarterly,* LXXIX (June, 1964), pp. 233–247; A. L. Horelick, "Cuban Missile Crisis: An Analysis of Soviet Calculations and Behavior," *World Politics,* XVI (April, 1964), pp. 363–389; and Dudley Seers, ed., *Cuba: The Economic and Social Revolution* (Chapel Hill, 1964). From the sociological angle, Maurice Zeitlin, *Revolutionary Politics and the Cuban Working Class* (Princeton, 1967), and José Yglesias, *In the Fist of the Revolution: Life in a Cuban Country Town* (New York, 1968), give valuable insights. Perhaps in the 1970s the United States and Cuba will renew diplomatic ties, and antagonisms may lessen in a new rapprochement. Until then, the objective historical record will not be written.

2 3 4 5 6 7 8 9 10